Paul Auster and the Influence of Maurice Blanchot

MARÍA LAURA ARCE

McFarland & Company, Inc., Publishers

Jefferson, North Carolina

ISBN (print) 978-1-4766-6361-6
ISBN (ebook) 978-1-4766-2490-7

LIBRARY OF CONGRESS CATALOGUING-IN-PUBLICATION DATA

BRITISH LIBRARY CATALOGUING DATA ARE AVAILABLE

Front cover image of open book © 2016 AOS82/iStock

Printed in the United States of America

*McFarland & Company, Inc., Publishers
Box 611, Jefferson, North Carolina 28640
www.mcfarlandpub.com*

To my parents,
Alicia and Héctor

Table of Contents

Acknowledgments

I would like to acknowledge the help of a number of people and organizations in the research and writing of this book and must begin with Professor Eulalia Piñero Gil for her enthusiasm, commitment and professionalism. This work could not have been possible without her help. I am also indebted to Elisabetta Marino and Rodica Mihaila for the time they dedicated to it. I would like to thank Françoise Delaunay for her excellent translations of Maurice Blanchot's letters.

This research took me to many libraries, and the present work could not have been possible without the help I received along the way. I am particularly grateful to Anne Garner, librarian in charge of the Paul Auster archive in the Berg Collection at the New York Public Library in July 2009. I would also like to thank Paul Auster who came with me to the library and guided me through his documents. Grateful acknowledgement is made to Cidalia Fernandes Blanchot, Eric Hoppenot, Isaac Gerwirtz and the Henry W. and Albert A. Berg Collection of English and American Literature, the New York Public Library, Astor, Lennox and Tilden Foundations for permission to reproduce a translation of Maurice Blanchot's letters to Paul Auster, June 4, 1975; December 28, 1975; August 21, 1981; and undated in the Paul Auster Papers, 1963–1995 (bulk 1972 through mid–1995); Miscellaneous Incoming Correspondence, Box 30 Folder 2 B. This material has been fundamental for the accomplishment of this work.

I am grateful to my family, Mariana, Guille, Tía Susi, Ceci, Pancho, Carol, Caro and Emi, for their love and patience with all my stories about Paul Auster.

I am thankful to my friends Belén Espiniella, Florencia Guillén, Elena Clemente, Jorge Castro and Óscar Curieses for their beautiful friendship, confidence, encouragement and constant trust in everything I do.

Introduction

Paul Auster's fiction is inscribed by the scholars in the American postmodern literary movement. Whereas part of contemporary American fiction is distinguished for defining a new wave of multicultural studies, Auster's literature manifests its postmodernity in a different way. Thus, he belongs to a group of writers whose fiction becomes a manifestation of a late modernism that questions the role of the writer and the function of language in the literary space. According to Malcom Bradbury, postmodern writing in the late 1980s "began to look with greater care at its relations to reality" (*American Novel* 257). In this particular context, Bradbury introduces Auster's fiction and asserts:

> If "reality" was, as Nabokov had said, a word that meant nothing except in quotes, and if once "realism" and "experiment" had been flags raised by camps at war, they now increasingly engaged in peaceful intercourse and profitable trade, and therefore Jerome Klinkowitz came up with his useful formulation "experimental realism." A good example of this trend is Paul Auster, a writer who, along with Walter Abish and Leonard Michaels, can be seen as a distinguished later contributor to what could now well be called "the postmodern tradition" [257].

In its origin, criticism in general characterizes Auster's fiction as a questioning and recreation of detective fiction. Certainly, Auster opens his fiction by presenting a new genre called anti-detective fiction in which the detective case in itself loses its track and aim in order to propose some existential issues. Together with this, Auster reflects, in most of his works, on the figure of the writer and the process of creation, sometimes framed in the context of an anti-detective fiction, sometimes presented in other contexts. In this way, Auster's deconstruction of detective fiction comes from the evident influence of authors like Edgar Allan Poe, the American fiction of the fifties and hard-boiled detective stories. However, the aim of this work is to focus on another specific critical link that has been barely studied by American literature academics. It is evident that there is a strong literary connection between the French writers and Paul Auster. This bond comes not only from literary curiosity but also from his stay in France and his involvement with French literature during the 1970s.

As a way of earning a living, Paul Auster developed his skills as a translator and he had the chance to study in depth some authors that were already an inspiration for his poetry and would have an effect on his future fiction. Among these writers, one name stands out: the French writer, philosopher and literary critic Maurice Blanchot. Auster's work with French writers had been very well known and his *The Random House Book of Twentieth-Century French Poetry* (1982) was a very valuable collection of French poetry. In it, Auster makes a selection of French poets including those he translated and other influential French poets of the twentieth century. In the preface of this anthology, he writes about the importance French poetry and literature have on American literature and concludes: "It is not simply that French must be considered an 'influence' on the development of English language and literature; French is a part of English, an irreducible element of its genetic make-up" (*Red Notebook* 41).

Apart from this, Auster, together with his first wife, the writer Lydia Davis, translated some fictional works and essays of the French writer Maurice Blanchot. Initiated by Davis, this project made it possible for Auster to approach two of Blanchot's short stories, "The Idyll" and "The Last Word," and the essay "After the Fact," all published in *The Station Hill Blanchot Reader* (1999). However, Paul Auster's first contact with Maurice Blanchot was with the translation of the essay "The Book of Questions" in 1971, about Edmond Jabès.

Rather than focusing the analysis on the anti-detective genre and the existential aspects it presents, I introduce the possible relationship the translation of Maurice Blanchot's texts and particularly his ars poetica could have to the construction of Paul Auster's fiction. The translated texts became for Auster his contact with Blanchot's critical theory and fiction. In the process of his translation, Auster exchanged some letters with Blanchot to certify and improve his translation.[1] Auster made it possible for me to have access to his archive in the New York Public Library and there I found all the letters he exchanged with Blanchot. These letters show evidence that Auster was interested in Blanchot reading his work and, in fact, Blanchot makes some comments on

Auster's poetry. This work takes this event as the starting point of a literary connection that is reflected in most of Auster's work. Although there is no evidence that Auster has been at some point familiarized with the whole of Blanchotian corpus, it is possible to track some basic concepts and theories proposed by the French philosopher in Auster's fiction. In other words, Blanchot's texts inspired Auster to fictionalize his theory of literature in his works.

Despite most of the criticism being centered on researching Auster's metafiction, intertextuality, existentialism, the use of language and the reinvention of literary genres, not many critics have focused their studies on the impact French literature and concretely French philosophy has had on Paul Auster's literary oeuvre. Certainly, critics such as Allison Russell in her essay "Deconstructing *The New York Trilogy*: Paul Auster's Anti-Detective Fiction" (1990) propose an interpretation of the trilogy from a Derridean perspective. Besides, Ilana Shiloh in her book *Paul Auster and Postmodern Quest: On the Road to Nowhere* (2002) uses Jean Paul Sartre's definition of existentialism in order to propose a reading of the issues of identity in the trilogy. Generally speaking, most of the critics point out the importance French writers have on Auster's corpus but not particularly Maurice Blanchot's effect on the American author's work. There are two writers who have worked closer to this thesis. Firstly, Jeffrey T. Nealon gives an interpretation of the first novel of the trilogy using part of Maurice Blanchot's theory of literature in his article "Work of the Detective, Work of the Writer: Paul Auster's *City of Glass*" (1996). In fact, Nealon asserts that Blanchot is present in this fiction as far as Quinn's work as a writer is depicted as the transition to a space of negation that is a metaphysical world. That is to say, the space of literature.

Secondly, Tom Theobald in his book *Existentialism and Baseball: The French Philosophical Roots of Paul Auster* (2010) proposes a thorough thesis about the relationship between Maurice Blanchot and Paul Auster. He presents what he calls "Auster's Blanchotian Anti-Canon" (189), a section in which he traces the original links between the American writer and the French philosopher, especially in the translated texts, which is an analysis also proposed in this work. Together with this, he points out different characteristics transformed and assimilated by Auster in his fiction. Concretely he asserts:

3

> Like Blanchot, Auster believes in literature as an anonymous sphere resistant to authority, and in writing as a commitment to the unknown and to ambiguity [...]. This idea that the book withdraws from the author, that it gains an onto-logical reality independent of the writer, is profoundly Blanchotian. Like Blanchot, Auster continually engages with the actual experience of writing [195].

Theobald applies Blanchot's theory to Auster's poetry and to his sixth novel *Leviathan* (1992). In the case of his poetry, it seems that Theobald focuses on the creation of a literary space through writing. Actually, he states, "The most obviously Blanchotian element of 'White Spaces' is its awareness of writing as a movement through a space opened up by writing itself" (197). On the other hand, *Leviathan* seems for Theobald a clear example of Blanchot's alterity, the idea of death and consequently the representation of the process of writing. As far as I am concerned, there are no other critical works that have dedicated an extensive analysis to the effect Maurice Blanchot's theory of litera-ture has had on Auster's oeuvre, especially with regards to the novels discussed in this work.

The aim of this comparative analysis is to study the Blanchotian concept of inspiration in Paul Auster's fiction as a fundamental step in the process of creation. In this context, Auster's work is studied as a fictionalization of Blanchot's poetics and concretely as a literary illus-tration of Blanchot's concept of inspiration. In order to do this, I work with Blanchot's main theoretical work *The Space of Literature*[2] (1955). In it, Maurice Blanchot introduces the most important points of his theory of literature in relation to the construction of literary space, the function of language in it, the role of the writer and the process of inspiration that takes place before and in it. Apart from this essential work, there are other works by the French philosopher in which the concept of inspiration is studied, such as *Faux Pas*[3] (1943), *The Work of Fire*[4] (1949), *The Book to Come*[5] (1959) or *The Infinite Conversation*[6] (1969). In this context, I deal with the second volume of *The New York Trilogy* (1987) titled *Ghosts* (1986), a novel several times criticized but never in comparison to Maurice Blanchot, and two novels whose lit-erary criticism is scarce: *The Music of Chance* (1990) and *Mr. Vertigo* (1994).

Ghosts is the story of a detective who has to watch someone whose only activity is to write the whole day. This simple occupation becomes a process of inspiration in which one is the creator while the other becomes the object created. The space left between them is what Blanchot calls the "orphic space." The second example shows how two individuals can be manipulated as puppets for a particular purpose. In *The Music of Chance*, it is the construction of an absurd wall which has no apparent utility that turns into a metaphor for depicting the process of inspiration that creates an entire imaginary world. The same occurs in the novel *Mr. Vertigo* in which a man trains a child to teach him how to fly. In the process of this training, the child is transformed into a different person and therefore the piece of art of his master. In order to reach to this final product, Auster shows how the child is an inspiration for the master and also how the child looks for his own inspiration to become what his master desires. The three novels, and the relationship of the characters with their manipulators or masters, are an example of Blanchot's thesis about Orpheus and Eurydice. That is, the French philosopher explains the inspirational connection between the creator and the object invented by the Greek myth of Orpheus and his desperate loss of Eurydice during his performance with the harp in the underworld. Through this myth, Blanchot formulates his theory of inspiration and Auster takes this to reformulate it in these two novels avoiding the role of the writer or the process of writing and putting all the attention on the instant of inspiration.

1

Paul Auster and Maurice Blanchot

An Intertextual Relation

The Translator as Writer: Intertextuality as a Framework of Influence

Intertextuality is a significant literary tool in Auster's work. From the first lines of *The New York Trilogy* (1987) characters' names are borrowed from other writers such as Edgar Allan Poe or Nathaniel Hawthorne. Even his own characters jump from one text to the other. He will repeat this technique in almost all his novels. In the introduction to her work *The World That Is the Book* (2001), Aliki Varvogli defends an approach of Auster's work in which intertextuality plays a very important role. In order to discuss this thesis, she argues: "The 'intertext' exists independently of the author's will, and it shapes both the production and the reception of any cultural artifact" (Varvogli 14). She proposes an analysis of all the different intertextual theories of the 20th century and concludes that

> when Paul Auster refers to Thoreau's *Walden,* he does not send his readers back to the book *Walden* written by Henry David Thoreau, but to the book Auster has read and then inscribed into his own text (and which is in turn decoded by the reader), and also to the mythic status the book has acquired even for those who, like Auster's character Blue, did not have the patience to read it. *Walden* in *Ghosts* is not the same as *Walden* in Thoreau, a book we can find in the library or bookshop. So we return to the *thematisation* of the intertext, which can be seen more clearly in Auster's later novels, where the emphasis moves away from individual authors and works to take into account the larger intertext of politics, history, and myth-making as systems of signification [18].

Undoubtedly, Varvogli proposes a "thematisation of the intertext," in which the reference introduced turns into one of the basic elements for the understanding and interpretation of the work. In this sense, Auster plays with several intertexual references in his novels that can be considered essential elements to form a system of significance. Apart from these external references, Auster also constructs his fiction by bringing into the text what can be considered an internal intertextuality. That is to say, some of Auster's characters travel across his different novels, implying changes in the content and structure of the work.

There is a third line of intertextuality in the case of Paul Auster which is the influence of his work as a translator in his fiction. Auster became a translator before starting his career as a published writer. It is well known, due to his non-fictional works,[1] that his experience as a translator was how he made a living during his years in Paris. In spite of this, it turned out to be an inflectional point in the construction of his poetics. Proof of that lies in his work *The Invention of Solitude* (1982), not only because it stands as what can be considered the theory that would shape his fiction, but also because it shows many of the intertextual references that justify his future work, including his translations. In this light, Mark Rudman, in his essay "Paul Auster: Some 'Elective Affinities,'" discusses the influence translations have had in Auster's work. He concludes:

> Auster identified, in the French writers he translated, kindred spirits, especially the writers of fragments. For the fragment is testimony to solitude; it sets in motion an investigation of fatality; it exists alone, with no before or after. Things remain on the cusp of knowing, of becoming [Rudman 44].

In this essay Rudman justifies the presence of solitude as a consequence of his work as a translator. In terms of Varvogli's internal intertextuality, there is only one direct reference to Maurice Blanchot in *The Invention of Solitude.* However, in his review of David Reed's painting, published in 1975, Paul Auster quotes Maurice Blanchot:

> In the last sentence of Maurice Blanchot's novel, *Death Sentence*, the nameless narrator writes: "And even more, let him try to imagine the hand that has written these pages: and if he is able to see it, then perhaps reading will become a serious task for him." David Reed's new work is an expression of this same desire in the realm of painting [Auster, *Collected Prose* 402].

Focusing on the words that Paul Auster chooses to quote, it is interesting how this quotation alludes to the act of reading and how it turns into something that affects his task as a writer. In his work *Exis-*

tentialism and Baseball: The French Philosophical Roots of Paul Auster Tom Theobald introduces what he calls "Auster's Blanchotian Anti-Canon" (Theobald 189). He discusses the connection between the American writer and the French philosopher due to the translations Paul Auster published at the beginning of his career. Together with this, he comments:

> The list of European writers that Auster admires or has written on his critical work is, in fact, astonishingly similar to that of Blanchot: Mallarmé, Kafka, Beckett, Joubert, Jabès, Rimbaud, and Hölderlin. Importantly, as in the case of Blanchot, these writers become transformed and assimilated into Auster's approach to writing and literature [189].

Here, Theobald presents a literary connection between Auster and Blanchot in terms of the authors that influenced them and, therefore, contributed to their literature. On the one hand, in the case of Blanchot, he uses these writers that Theobald mentions in order to create a theory of literature. Theobald comments in this respect: "Auster's conception of literature, delineated by his translations and critical work, relates to the domain of absence, fragmentation, solitude, silence and nothingness" (191). On the other hand, Auster uses the same authors to construct his fiction. Blanchot's influence on Auster comes from the practice of translation.

Auster's contact with Blanchot during a period of his life is evident, not only through his translations but also through a personal contact via letters in which Blanchot advices and orients him regarding the translation into English.[2] Moreover, the letters also reveal Auster's interest in having his books read by Blanchot and demonstrate how he expressed not only his gratitude but also his admiration for Auster's writing (Letter 1, 21 August 1981). It is relevant to bear in mind that up to that moment Auster had only published poetry; his first non-fictional work would come out in 1982.

As it is well known the term "intertextuality" was first coined by the French literary critic Julia Kristeva to "designate the various relationships that a given text may have with other texts" (Baldick 112). However, despite the fact that Kristeva is considered the creator of this literary term, there are other authors who can be considered the precursors of the formulation of her theory. According to Chris Baldick, in his definition of intertextuality, "in the literary theories of structuralism and post-structuralism, texts are seen to refer to other texts (or to themselves as texts) rather than to an external reality" (112). In order to formulate her theory, Kristeva goes back to writers like Ferdinard de Saussure (1857–1913) and Mikhail Bakhtin (1895–1975). As Graham Allen asserts in his work *Intertextuality* (2000), Saussure is considered the originator of modern linguistics due to his work *Course in General Linguistics* (1915) in which he gives a definition for a linguistic sign (Allen 8). Essentially, Saussure proposes a thesis in which a linguistic sign would be formed by two parts: one would represent the concept, what he calls the signified, and the other the sound and image, what he calls the signifier. Together with this, and in relation to the interaction of individuals, Saussure proposes an analysis of language divided into *parole* and *langage*, understanding *langage* as speech and *parole* as the act of utterance (Allen 17). In relation to Saussure, Allen focuses the attention on the idea of the differential sign as the essence for a definition of intertextuality. As he explains:

> For Saussure, the linguistic sign is not simply arbitrary, it is also differential. [...] The placing of words together in sentences involves what is termed the syntagmatic (combinatory) axis of language; the selection of certain words out of possible words involves what is termed the paradigmatic (selection) axis of language [9].

Through this idea, Saussure establishes a linguistic system in which the sign is the object of many different relationships, that, in the end, constitute what he calls the "synchronic system of language" (Allen 11). In other words, linguistic signs have meaning since they belong to a linguistic system in a specific moment of time that establishes connections with other signs inside that system. In this way, Graham Allen explains the relationship between Saussure's theory and intertextuality in the following terms:

> Authors of literary works do not just select words from a language system, they select plots, generic features, aspects of character, images, ways of narrating, even phrases and sentences from previous literary texts and from the literary tradition. If we imagine the literary tradition as itself a synchronic system, then the literary author becomes a figure working with at least two systems, those of language in general and of the literary system in particular. Such a point reinforces Saussure's stress on the non-referential nature of signs, since in reading literature we become intensely aware that the signs deployed in any particular text have their reference not to objects in the world but to the literary system out of which the text is produced [11].

In the extract above, Allen adapts the linguistic system to a literary system working in the act of writing creation. Therefore, he concludes that the behavior of signs in the language system is similar not to the one that occurs in the literary system but in the system itself as a traditional synchronic system. This is the reason why instead of choosing words, the author would choose, as Allen points out, "character, images, ways of narrating" as elements that conform the traditional system.

Contrary to Saussure's thesis, Mikhail Bakhtin does not believe in a synchronic system of language. One of his most relevant contributions to the definition of intertextuality is the social dimension of the linguistic system. That is to say, language is affected by the concrete social situation in which it is contextualized. Likewise, Bakhtin introduces a thesis that turns into one of the most fundamental ideas for Kristeva in the construction of her intertextual theory. The Russian critic coins the term "dialogism" to explain that "all utterances are dialogic, their meaning and logic dependent upon what has previously been said and on how they will be received by others" (Allen 19). Compared to this hypothesis, the Saussurean linguistic system is a monologic one in which utterances work as independent entities deprived of any social or ideological relationship. Thus, it is evident the interconnections between one specific utterance to others inside the text and outside of it make the existence of intertextual references possible.

According to Bakhtin, the novel represents a dialogical space where one discourse can be influenced by another which can refer to other aspects that affect language or other traditional discourses. In his essay "From the Prehistory of Novelistic Discourse" (1967), Bahktin expresses it in the following way:

> We speak of a special novelistic discourse because it is only in the novel that discourse can reveal all its specific potential and achieve its true depth. But the novel is a comparatively recent genre. Indirect discourse, however, the representation of another's world, another's language in intonational quotation marks, was known in the most ancient times; we encounter it in the earliest stages of verbal culture. What is more, long before the appearance of the novel we find a rich world of diverse forms that transmit, mimic and represent from various vantage points another's word, another's speech and language, including also the languages of the direct genres [Lodge 132].

Bakhtin constructs his theory of dialogism based on what he calls the polyphonic novel, that is, a novel in which many discourses come together in the fictional space and all of them unavoidably refer to other discourses (Allen 23). Besides, Bahktin studies the idiosyncrasy of the polyphonic novel by analyzing two discourses that collide in a dialogue and he calls the "double-voiced discourse," an idea he will specify in the concept of heteroglosia (Allen 28). Through this thesis Kristeva formulates her theory of intertextuality.

In her work *Desire in Language: A Semiotic Approach to Literature and Art* (1969), Julia Kristeva formulates what is considered the first definition for a thesis of intertextuality. Her starting point is Bakhtin's idea of heteroglosia and the fact that a text is constructed from other texts. Therefore, texts are not separated from the ideological and cultural context they exist in; indeed discourses are formed in this social and ideological context. The key idea in Kristeva's proposal for a definition of intertextuality consists in considering the text a productivity. The French linguist explains it in the following way:

> first, that its relationship to the language in which it is situated is redistributive (destructive-constructive), and hence can be better approached through logical categories rather than linguistic ones; and second, that it is a permutation of texts, an intertextuality: in the space of a given text, several utterances, taken from other texts, intersect and neutralize one another [Kristeva 36].

In order to explain her theory about how a text does not only depend on itself but also on other aspects external to it, and therefore to concretize her definition of this new concept of "intertextuality," Kristeva introduces the idea of ideologeme. According to Kristeva, "the ideologeme is the intersection of a given textual arrangement (a semiotic practice) with the utterances (sequences) that it either assimilates into its own space or to which it refers in the space of exterior texts (semiotic practices)" (36). In other words, the text, from this intertextual perspective, is inserted in a social and historical background. Thus, the text moves from the particular, as a text that has a meaning in itself, to the general in which it gains meaning inside a social and historical frame. Furthermore, Kristeva explains how the concept of ideologeme works in a novel as a text and she concludes: "the functions defined according to the extra-novelistic textual set (Te) take on value within the novelistic textual set (Tn). The ideologeme of the novel is precisely this *intertextual* function defined according to Te and having value within Tn" (37).

Still, Julia Kristeva continues with her analysis of the novel and concretely with the analysis of what she calls the "poetic meaning" as characteristic of the fictional discourse. In order to theorize about this,

Kristeva goes back to Mikhail Bakhtin again and analyzes his thesis about narrative structure. In relation to this, Kristeva states, "Bakhtin was one of the first to replace the static hewing out of texts with a model where literary structure does not simply *exist* but is generated in relation to *another* structure" (65). Based on Bakhtin's concept of dialogism, Kristeva presents three different layers in the literary space formed by what she calls the "poetic word" (65):

> These three dimensions or coordinates of dialogue are writing subject, addressee, and exterior texts. The word's status is thus defined *horizontally* (the word in the text belongs to both writing subject and addressee) as well as *vertically* (the word in the text is oriented toward an anterior or synchronic literary corpus) [66].

Here is the essence of the theory of intertextuality since, as Kristeva concludes, the coincidence of these two axes brings up a relevant thesis: "each word (text) is an intersection of word (texts) where at least one other word (text) can be read" (66). In this context, Kristeva reflects on what can be the basic contribution for her theory of intertextuality: "any text is the absorption and transformation of another. The notion of *intertextuality* replaces that of intersubjectivity, and poetic language is read as at least *double*" (66).

In the construction of her theory of intertextuality, Julia Kristeva, apart from Mikhail Bakhtin, considers essential the work of Roland Barthes.[3] One of the most significant contributions of Roland Barthes in relation to intertextuality is the distinction between the concept of work and the concept of text. The work, apart from representing meaning, communication and authorial skills, mainly represents an object for Barthes. On the other hand, the idea of text fundamentally stands for the process of writing. As he claims in his essay "From Work to Text":

> The text is a process of demonstration, speaks according to certain rules (or against certain rules); the work can be held in the hand, the text is held in language, only exists in the movement of a discourse (or rather, it is Text for the very reason that it knows itself as text); the Text is not the decomposition of the work, it is the work that is the imaginary tail of the Text; or again, *the Text is experienced only in an activity of production.* It follows that the Text cannot stop (for example on a library shelf); its constitutive movement is that of cutting across (in particular, it can cut across the work, several works) [Barthes, *Image* 162].

Since Barthes considers the text as a productive space, and remarks "the Text is experienced only in an activity of production," the idea of plurality clearly defines this linguistic space in terms of a "weave of signifiers." In other words, the text is constructed as a woven fabric in which signifiers are chained and therefore refer to other signifiers. Certainly, this is what Barthes calls intertextuality:

> The intertextual in which every text is held, it itself being the text-between of another text, is not to be confused with some origin of the text: to try to find the "sources," the "influences" of a work, is to fall in with the myth of filiation; the citations which go to make up a text are anonymous, untraceable, and yet *already read*: they are quotations without inverted commas [Barthes, *Image* 165].

Thus, whereas Kristeva proposes the intersection of different texts since these texts or words are at the same time the assimilation and transformation of another (66), Barthes proposes a plurality based on the strong connection of signifiers in the space of the text.

In one of these reflections about Kristeva's and Barthes's works, Graham Allen establishes a connection between their theories and the transition to modernism and postmodernism. In this sense, he concludes:

> It would appear that for Barthes, as for Kristeva, only Modernist and Postmodernist literature give us examples of the *text*; examples, that is, of texts which, because they self consciously put into play the power of the signifier and of writing, can be re-written, rather than simply read, by the reader [65].

It is in this postmodernist context, in the light of the text considered "the power of the signifier and of writing," in which Paul Auster's fiction can be interpreted. If we regard Paul Auster's text as the interaction and combination of multiple signifiers that belong to a chain of infinite meanings, its connection with Blanchot becomes possible. Accordingly, Paul Auster's fiction turns into a transformation and assimilation of Blanchot's texts, among others. Certainly, the Auster-Blanchot connection not only comes from an explicit and concrete translating situation, but also through the experience with other writers such as Mallarmé, Kafka, Beckett, Joubert, Jabès, Rimbaud or Hölderlin. Undoubtedly, these authors, in the case of Auster and in the case of Blanchot, helped to create both the fiction and the critical work of the American writer and the French philosopher.

Auster's fiction is enclosed in an intertextual structure of different texts and authors, both external and internal. Nevertheless, Auster's influence comes unavoidably from his role as a translator. There is a connection between the act of translating and the effect that can have on the creativity of the translator in a possible role as writer. Susan Bassnett in her essay titled "Writing and Translating" included in the work *The Translator as Writer* edited by herself and Peter Bush claims that the act of translating is creative since

> translators are all the time engaging with texts first as readers and then as rewriters, as recreators of that text in another language. Indeed, given the constraint of having to work within the parameters of that source text, it could be argued that translation requires an extraordinary set of literary skills, no whit inferior to the skills required to produce that text in the first instance [Bassnett and Bush 174].

Here, Bassnett points out the literary and creative aspect of translation as a recreation of a text and therefore the formation of the translator as a writer. Besides, some lines after she states, "Translation, like imitation, can be a means of learning the craft of writing, for if writers can recognize and learn to speak in different voices it becomes more probable that they will identify a distinctive voice of their own" (174). Thus translation and imitation imply a way of learning writing skills. Linked to this, it is remarkable that in the same way translation is compared to imitation in its origin, so is intertextuality. In other words, intertextuality is originally a way of imitating. In the book *Intertextuality: Theory and Practices*, Michael Worton and Judith Still start their definition of intertextuality by presenting Aristotle's thesis in his *Poetics* and they assert:

> Aristotle holds that we learn through imitating others and that our instinct to enjoy works of imitation is inborn instinct; both Cicero and Quintilian emphasize that imitation is not only a means of forging one's own discourse but is a consciously intertextual practice [6].

In relation to this, Lawrence Venuti in his article "Translation, Intertextuality and Interpretation" proposes a thesis in which the translator, in his role as writer, creates an intertextual relationship between the two texts through a process of recreation as Bassnett asserts. Venuti explains:

> The translator creates an intertextual relation by reproducing a pre-existing text in the translating language, whether specifically through quotation or more generally through imitation of its graphemes and sound, lexicon and syntax, style and discourse. [...] A translation then recontextualizes both the foreign text that it translates and the translating-language text that it quotes or imitates, submitting them to a transformation that changes their significance [165].

15

The encounter between these two disciplines, translating and inter-textuality, occurs in the figure of the translator. Furthermore, the act of translating has as one of its immediate consequences a process of intertextuality that directly affects and reshapes the role of the translator as writer. Auster illustrates very well this influence in the following quotation from his work *The Invention of Solitude* (1982):

> For most of his adult life, he has earned his living by translating the books of other writers. He sits at his desk reading the book in French and then picks up his pen and writes the same book in English. It is both the same book and not the same book, and the strangeness of this activity has never failed to impress him. Every book is an image of solitude. [...] A sits down in his own room to translate another man's book, and it is as though he were entering that man's solitude and making it his own. [...] A imagines himself as a kind of ghost of that other man, who is both there and not there, and whose book is both the same and not the same as the one he is translating. Therefore, he tells himself, it is possible to be alone and not alone at the same moment [Auster, *Solitude* 136].

Paul Auster started his work as a translator in 1971, with an uncred-ited translation of the essay "Miró as Sculpture" written by Jacques Dupin. This translation was published in the first edition of an art catalogue in Minneapolis by the Walker Art Center. From 1971 to 1982 he combines his work as a poet with his work as a translator and an editor. The year 1982 was very important for Auster's career as a writer because that is the year in which two of his most important texts of nonfiction, *The Art of Hunger* (1982) and *The Invention of Solitude*, were published. These essays, together with others that will come afterwards, constitute Auster's ars poetica for his future fiction. Indeed, not only these texts but also his poems helped him to develop a theory of literature specific to his fiction. However, before that, in 1972, there is evidence of the first published con-tact between Auster and Blanchot's work. He published in the journal of *European Judaism* (v. 12) a translation of Blanchot's essay "Edmond Jabès' Book of Questions." Subsequently, in 1975, he edited, together with Lydia Davis, issue number 4 of *Living Hand*, with texts by Maurice Blanchot, Larry Eigner, Hugh Seidman, Sarah Plimpton, Lydia Davis, Anthony Bar-nett, Russell Edson and Rosmarie Waldrop. It would be 1985 when Paul Auster got involved in a project to translate two short stories and a critical essay written by Blanchot. The texts were published under the title *Vicious Circles: Two Fictions & "After the Fact"* and included in a collection of Blanchot's texts called *The Station Hill Blanchot Reader* (1985).

16

As far as anyone can prove, Auster approached Blanchot's work as an editor and translator. According to William Denttrel and his book *Paul Auster: A Comprehensive Bibliographic Checklist of Published Works 1968–1994*, Paul Auster's first contact with Blanchot's texts was in 1971 when he translated Blanchot's essay "The Book of Questions" on Edmond Jabès. Later on, this essay was published in a book which collects a number of texts written by Blanchot titled *Friendship* (1997), translated by Elizabeth Rottenberg and published by Stanford University Press. "The Book of Questions" is Blanchot's analysis and a reflection on the book written by Edmond Jabès with the same title. From Blanchot's point of view, "The Book of Questions" is about the relationship between the act of writing and Judaism. This idea moved Blanchot to write a thesis about writing's intimate relationship with interruption and consequent fragmentation. As a matter of fact, what Blanchot does is develop his idea about interruption in writing using Jabès's text in order to support his argument. The following quotation expresses Blanchot's idea:

> In the totality of fragments, thoughts, dialogues, invocations, narrative move-
> ments, and scattered words that make up the detour of a single poem, I find
> the powers of interruption at work, so that the writing, and what is proposed
> to writing (the uninterrupted murmur, what does not stop), must be accom-
> plished in the act of interrupting itself [Blanchot, *Friendship* 222–223].

So, in this way, Blanchot states that Jabès's work always questions the interruption and fracture that takes place in both the act of writing and history and, this idea allows him to introduce a consecutive argument that explains how the creation of the book takes place in the movement of this fracture.

Paul Auster had the chance to interview Edmond Jabés on November 4, 1978, at Keith and Rosemarie Waldrop's house. This interview was possible thanks to Edmond Jabès's long reading tour of the United States during that time. Some of the extracts and comments of this interview give light and clarify several points explained by Blanchot in the essay. Besides, as the interviewer, Auster becomes the link between Jabès and Blanchot.[4] Apart from expressing his opinions regarding language, he connects his ideas with Blanchot's. Auster observes that Jabès explains that communication between people can only happen in the form of questions. In order to formulate his argument, Jabès quotes Blanchot and concludes:

Because ... and it was Blanchot who noticed this in an article for the NRF published in 1964 ... because when two people talk, one of them must always remain silent. We are talking now, for example, and as I am saying these words you are forced to remain silent. If we both spoke at the same time, neither one of us could hear what the other was saying. Now, during this silence that you impose on yourself, you are all the time forming questions and answers in your mind, since you can't keep interrupting me. And as I continue to speak, you are eliminating questions from your mind: all you say to yourself, that's what he meant, all right. But if I went on speaking for a long time and we went away before you had a chance to reply? When we met again, you wouldn't come back with an answer, you would come back with a question [Auster, *Interview* 10–11].

With his intervention, Jabès explains his theory about interruption but from another perspective. This time, it is linked with language and concretely with silence, a concept that will be very important for Blanchot's corpus. Here, Jabès talks about an invisible interruption, a fracture that stays in silence and that comes back to its origin, which was, according to Jabès's example, the question.

An Epistolary Friendship: The Letters of Blanchot to Auster

In 1985, a collection of fiction and literary essays by Blanchot was published under the title *The Station Hill Blanchot Reader*. In it, Paul Auster translated two pieces of fiction, "The Idyll" and "The Last Word," and a literary essay titled "After the Fact," which is a reflection of Blanchot himself in relation to the previous two short stories. The three texts were published as *Vicious Circles: Two Fictions & "After the Fact."* This is Auster's big contribution to Blanchot's texts in English and also the most important influence that Auster will receive for his poetry, fiction and non-fiction. Although there are evident signs of Blanchot's theory in non-fiction works published before the translation of these texts (*The Invention of Solitude* or *The Art of Hunger* are non-fiction texts in which Blanchot's theory can be traced and were published in 1981), they acted as guides for following novels published from 1987 onwards. The most significant evidence of the literary and personal relationship between Paul Auster and Maurice Blanchot are the four letters sent by Maurice Blanchot to Paul Auster between 1975 and 1981 in response to some doubts and comments related to the translations the American writer was working on at the same time.[5] The first one dated June 4, 1975, is focused on discussing the translation of the text *L'Arrêt de mort* published in France in 1948 by Editions Gallimard and later on in the volume *The Station Hill Blanchot Reader* in 1999.

48 rue Madame
75006 Paris
4th of June 1975

Dear Paul Auster,

Thank you for this translation that I find excellent (as far as I can judge it) and I thank Lydia Davis as well. But may you allow me to raise the problem of the title? Death Halt disappoints me and also disappoints competent people. I know that there is a problem with it. That is the double meaning (at least, double) of the French title: death halted, suspended but even pronounced: the death sentence. In the translations to the German or Italian language, we have always had to innovate around this title, more or less successfully. How can we restitute, communicate the feeling, the ambiguous and mysterious attraction of "L'arrêt de mort," a name that even for me remains enigmatic?

I wonder if you are in America or in France. I write to you in America. Please give my best regards to Lydia Davis and my fondest thoughts for you.

Maurice Blanchot

The letter focuses mainly on the linguistic problem the title translated into English brings. Apparently, the French writer is not happy with Auster's and Davis's choice and suggests a change. In all the letters, the figure of Lydia Davis, Auster's first wife, is present and seems an active participant in the translations. Another letter with no date but which goes on discussing the same translation, complements this letter.

21, Place des Pensées
78320 Le Mesnil Saint-Denis

Dear Paul Auster,

I really like your review, and I give you my permission for the publishing of the 1st part of "L'Arrêt de Mort" (nevertheless don't forget to mention that this is only the first part).

Let's keep in touch.
With my fondest thoughts,

Maurice Blanchot

This second letter shows more literary contact between the two writers—that is, it seems that Auster sent Blanchot a review of some of his works. Together with this, he gives permission to publish the first part of the work finally translated by Lydia Davis, *Death Sentence*, and he gives some specific instructions on how to do so. Indeed, in the Station Hill edition, in the notes on *Death Sentence*, Lydia Davis adds: "This translation follows the first edition of *L'Arrête de Mort* (1948). In the Second Edition (1971), the brief final section was deleted by the author" (Blanchot, *Station Hill* 504). In a third letter which seems following the one quoted above, Maurice Blanchot suggests the way in which they can clarify the change of his text in the 1971 edition and he gives the exact instructions followed by Lydia Davis.

> Paris, on the 28th of December
>
> Dear Paul Auster,
>
> I would propose the following solution: translate the last page according to the 1948 edition and indicate in a bottom of page note, that, in a recent edition, this page disappeared (or else the opposite, make it your choice: translate the last page in an added note, although this seems to me to be more sophisticated—but again, do as you feel).
>   I send you as well my kindest regards and all my wishes for your work and your life,
>
> Maurice Blanchot

In the fourth and last letter, dated August 21, 1981, Blanchot openly feels grateful for Auster's work with his text and especially happy with the choice of the title in English. Also, he again mentions Lydia Davis as the person who opened the doors of America to him and he seems very aware of the fact that thanks to her, he is known there. Remarkably, he flatters Auster's poetic work and he explicitly says that he felt "touched" by his poems. Moreover, he even uses one of his theoretical terms to define Auster's poems and says that "poetry remains the inaccessible essential," an expression that would be present throughout Auster's fiction. Taking into account that there are no more letters sent to Auster in the Paul Auster archive at the Berg Collection, it is possible that this is the last letter that Maurice Blanchot sent to the American writer and therefore the end of their correspondence. In spite of this, the French writer always seemed very open maintaining a relationship and always sounded very kind and willing to help Auster as it shows in this last letter.

> 21st of August 1981
> 21, Place des Pensées
> 78320 Le Mesnil Saint Denis
>
> Dear Paul Auster,
>
> It is only today that I was given your address through Christian Miller (of Station Hill Press), whom I had asked for it as soon as I received Vicious Cir-

cles (very good title by the way), wanting to let you know how grateful I felt for the translation of these narratives that were, if I remember well, the first ones I wrote (with no intention at all of being published). The Susan Quasha's presentation is plain and impressive.

I would like, of course, to hear from you. You know how much Lydia dedicated her time and talent (even sacrificing her own personal work) to make accessible several of my narratives and essays, which, if it was not for her, would not have crossed the oceans, like (in imitation of) the big pilgrims of the May Flower.

I do not know if I mentioned to you how much I was touched by your poems; poetry remains the inaccessible essential.

Truly yours, with my faithful friendship,

Maurice Blanchot

Blanchot's Vicious Circles: Two Fictions & "After the Fact"

The text titled in English *Vicious Circles: Two Fictions & "After the Fact"* is the only fiction texts written by Maurice Blanchot translated by Auster. Essentially, different aspects and themes that shape the plot and characters of the two fictional stories can be traced in Blanchot's theory of literature. At the same time, these aspects will enlighten Auster's fiction in some particular cases. The essay titled "After the Fact" was published in 1951 as an extension of the edition of *Le Ressassement éternel*. This study is composed of three parts: first, a general discussion about the role of the writer, and two other parts, each dedicated to the analysis of "The Idyll" and "The Last Word." In the first part of the essay, he refers to an expression *Noli me legere*, a sentence that will become the title of a section in his future book *The Space of Literature* (1955). If the stories cover language, space and essential solitude, this essay deals with the figure of the writer and the relationship with his creation.

The first story of the two titled *Vicious Circles* is "The Idyll," subtitled by Blanchot as "The Idyll or the Torment of the Happy Idea" (1936). It is situated in a dystopia in which the main activity is to prepare the immigrant before he or she is ready to be integrated into a new society itself. The central character, Alexander Akim, undergoes this training. Of course, there are two spaces: the "Home" which is the place that prepares strangers for their new society and the new society.

As the story shows, there is a strong contrast between the "Home," which would stand for the locked place where a number of individuals cohabit, and the exterior world, that is completely prohibited for them and which they long to know. The protagonist, rather than immersing himself in his process of transformation, is desperate to recuperate his freedom and get lost in the city. Parallel to this story, the writer introduces two important characters: the boss of the "House" and his wife, a couple who seems to be very happy even though everybody else in the "House" questions their happiness. In an attempt to be released and to imitate his boss's happiness, he decides to get married. Marriage, according to the laws of the house, was a strategy to get out of the house since it was considered a way of integrating into society. Nevertheless, the protagonist, unable to control his desire of seeing and feeling the city, goes out before his marriage and is killed by the members of the "House," as its laws dictate.

The protagonist, at the beginning, is introduced as a stranger and as a vagabond. Concretely, he says, "I'm only a vagabond. I don't have time to observe people" (Blanchot, *Station Hill* 8). If we compare this text with Auster's first fiction, both narratives share the fact that the protagonist is a vagabond or suffers a progressive transformation into that figure. This happens in novels like *The New York Trilogy*, *In the Country of Last Things*, *Moon Palace*, *Timbuktu* and even *Leviathan*, in which protagonists are more than vagabonds; they live a very precarious life due to their condition as outsiders and criminals. In addition, this experience sometimes goes together with a temporary and voluntary rejection of food, which results, at the end, in a slow disintegration of the individual. Nonetheless, there is one thing that distinguishes Auster's hobo from Blanchot's: Blanchot's does not have time to observe people whereas a crucial feature of Auster's is that he is always an observer. Actually, Auster's hobo desolation is in part caused because they focus all of their energies on observing the lives of others. In spite of this general attitude, it is true that sometimes their desolation is provoked by the social setting, as occurs in *In the Country of Last Things*.

If Blanchot starts playing with the figure of the stranger, he continues with the concept of identity in order not to abandon the definition of the individual. Both concepts, stranger and identity, are intimately related and confront the protagonist with the external society. In the story, the central character seems not to have a name; apparently, he is given a name by the boss's wife: "'Well, see you soon, Alexander Akim.' This strange name suited him as well as any other: he was no more than a kind of a beggar here" (Blanchot, *Station Hill* 9). This quotation shows an ambiguity the reader is not able to solve and it is not clear if that is the protagonist's name or, on the contrary, the name that the "House" gives him. In any case, the reassignment of a new name, which in a way represents the assignation of a new identity, is part of the process of transforming the protagonist into a new person and particularly, the proper person to fit into the new society.

In terms of Auster's fiction, identity is one of the aspects that becomes more important in the development of the plot. The transformation of Auster's characters into vagabonds can be interpreted as the disintegration of the self, but the American writer combines this theme with the idea of identity. His protagonists not only have doubles—other characters who resemble them psychologically and physically—but they also tend to impersonate others in an act of trying to erase their original identity and therefore become a different person. Thus, the link between the two writers is possible and the fusion of these three topics—homelessness, otherness and identity—blend in the sources of Auster's novels.

As soon as the protagonist is installed in the "House," he is forced to start hard labor which is part of the training he needs to become a suitable citizen. The narrator explains:

> Right after that, he was led to the quarry to work with the other men. They were supervised by a giant, a very ugly but good-natured person who was always agitated and upset. The work consisted of taking the stones that were dug out of the mountain each day by the city laborers and carting them to a huge pit. In the heat of the sun this was an exhausting task, exhausting and useless. Why throw the stones into this pit when special trucks would be coming afterwards to haul them away? [10].

In relation to the story, this passage has two interpretations. First of all, in his essay "After the Fact," Blanchot makes an analysis of his two fictions and openly writes about a possible comparison between this text and the Holocaust. Actually, he asserts that it is "a story from before Auschwitz. No matter when it is written, every story from now on will be from before Auschwitz" (Blanchot, *Station Hill* 495). Secondly, and linked to the condition of modern man and modern society, the passage can be interpreted as a new reading of the myth of Sisyphus. According to Greek mythology, Sisyphus was condemned to roll a rock up a hill that, once at the top, he let go of in order to start his job again. Both stories, Sisyphus's and Blanchot's, include seemingly useless activities but the narrative acquires a different perspective if we analyze it from the point of view of its absurdity and the condition of modern man.[6]

Blanchot states in his essay that the relationship between man and the world in the short story becomes absurd and it is in this bond that the individual gets lost and the search for the truth has no meaning (Blanchot, *Faux* 55). Thus, the story is a quest that remains unresolved. As he claims in "After the Fact":

> The story does not explain itself. If it is the tension of a secret around which it seems to elaborate itself and which immediately declares itself without being elucidated, it only announces its own movement, which can lay the groundwork for the game of deciphering and interpretation, but it remains a *stranger* to itself [Blanchot, *Station Hill* 493].

The aim of the story and even the characters's actions seem absurd and unfinished. Comparably, the characters of the American writer are trapped in these detective plots or awkward situations that do not have an original explanation or conclusive solution. In the concrete case of *The New York Trilogy*, the central characters are immersed in detective investigations that have no solution or in which the central character is unable to solve the mystery. Indeed, the reader can interpret it as a story with no real case at all, but a metaphor for something else.[7] Likewise, this idea can also be applied to *In the Country of Last Things*, a dystopia where the characters are completely lost in what seems a horrible and dangerous version of New York City. The protagonist, Anna Blume, is looking for her brother, a journalist who has disappeared without a trace. As the novel progresses, Anna focuses all of her energies in surviving and leaves her pursuit aside.

There is a negative perspective in this story—a chance of a life without hope—and it is at this point where Blanchot's and Auster's fiction overlap again. In this specific case, the similitude is established another time with the novel *In the Country of Last Things*. Although Blanchot's short story is not a dystopia, since he explicitly stated that it is not a "reading of an already menacing future" (493) it is a society that controls its inhabitants and emigrants, that prepares strangers to naturalize with the new environment in which they are not free; all this is done under the compliance of restrictive laws whose violation will be punished on pain of death. Bearing in mind these features, Auster's novel fits in the context and theme of "The Idyll." As a matter of fact, one of the most important aspects of the novel is freedom and how characters are condemned to live in this chaotic city in which there is no way to escape. Also, Anna, the protagonist, is a stranger, an immigrant who voluntarily has risked her life to live in that city for the purpose of finding her brother. Blanchot reflects on the idea of exile in relation to the story and he asserts:

> The exile cannot accommodate himself to his condition, nor to renouncing it, not to turning exile into a mode of residence. The immigrant is tempted to naturalize himself, through marriage for example, but he continues to be a migrant. In a place where there is no way out, to escape is the demand that restores the call of the outside [492].

For both characters, the final quest is for freedom. Alexander dies trying to be free and Anna is still attempting to free herself in the last lines of the novel. Likewise, Anna tries hard, unsuccessfully, to be part of this dystopia full of obstacles, terror and, of course, death.

"The Last Word" (1935), the second short story translated by Paul Auster, still moves in the same blurred atmosphere of "The Idyll" but, this time, it concerns the idea of language, the concept of solitude and reduced spaces. Like in "The Idyll," characters live in a strange city where language has been prohibited in such a way that most people do not speak and when they do, they normally forget what they have said. The central character moves around the plot trying to survive from that situation and without accepting the fact that he has to stop talking. In this context, the central theme of the story is language. First of all, the character is taken into an empty library, a metaphor for the absence of words, and from there, he is imprisoned in a cell with an old lady. The library's janitor talks to the protagonist in these terms:

> "Be quiet," he answered harshly. "This is the hour of solitude" and then he pushed me into a cell and carefully closed the door.
> There was a book lying open on the table apparently put there for me. Thinking I was alone, I was about to take a look at it when an old woman sleeping on some blankets in the corner let out a cry [38].

There are two basic elements in this passage that Blanchot will use in his theory of literature: solitude and the locked room, which in the short story is illustrated as a cell. If we put together the strange atmosphere of the city and the character of the old lady, it is possible to compare them with the character created by Auster in *In the Country of Last Things*, the old lady that will accompany Anna in the first part of the novel. Furthermore this library also resembles the library that appears almost at the end of Auster's novel. Nevertheless, for Anna and the rest of the characters that inhabit that library, it acts as a refuge from the hostile outside world, and this is why it was crowded with people. In this case, the library is empty, but it is as well a refuge for those who still use language.

Secondly, and blended with the other two aspects, language is represented in the image of a book. This is the first thing the protagonist sees in the cell. In it, he can read:

> There was a time when language no longer linked words according to simple relationships. It became such a delicate instrument that most people were forbidden to use it. But men naturally lack wisdom. The desire to be united through outlawed bonds never left them in peace, and they mocked this decree. In the face of such folly reasonable people decided to stop speaking. Those who had not been forbidden to speak who knew how to express themselves, resolved to stay silent from then on. They seemed to have learned words only to forget them. Associating them with what was most secret, they turned them away from their natural course [38].

The first sentence of this passage goes back to "The Book of Questions" and the fracture that exists between language and the world; in fact, the city and the prohibition to talk is a way of illustrating this idea. However, we can go one step further regarding Blanchot's theory of literature since we can find extracts in his book *The Space of Literature* that, in a way, mirror or clarify what the French philosopher wants to transmit:

> In crude or immediate speech, language as language is silent. But beings speak in it. And, as a consequence of the *use* which is its purpose-because, that is it serves primarily to put us in connection with objects, because it is a tool in a world of tools where what speaks is utility and value-beings speak in it as values [Blanchot, *Space* 40].

The narrator of the short story talks about speaking and not about an imaginary space, nonetheless Blanchot is pointing out all the different resources necessary to create a literary space. The cell, the book and language become three indispensable tools to start a process of writing creation, thus the whole story can be interpreted as a fictional representation of the imaginary space.

In the same way, these three elements become essential for some of Auster's novels. Rooms are recurrent and crucial spaces for the American writer's characters and plots. Together with the room, there is, most of the time, a character who takes the role of the writer. In *The New York Trilogy* or *Travels in the Scriptorium* (2006) characters live condemned to this activity. One of the novels that better combines these elements is *Travels in the Scriptorium*: the action is situated in a room, where an old writer waits for the visit of different guests, who happen to be the characters he has created. The writer has forgotten most of his life and is unable to use language, which is why his room is full of stickers with the names of the objects in them so he can identify them. This example can be interpreted as a way of fictionalizing Blanchot's theory of literature and, in this case, it also resembles the plot of "The Last Word."

Language is also expressed in relation to the city. At some point in the story the character is locked in the cell no longer and comes out to the city. The intention of the narrator is to express a projection to the exterior while establishing a connection with the urban space. The character expresses it this way:

> As we were walking down the streets, I took off my shoes and let myself be carried along by the crowd. It was pressing all around me. The cries came from a very deep place, they went through my body and came out of my mouth. I spoke without having to say a word [41].

The narrator describes a city language, as if only being outside would be an act of communication with no need to speak. Some lines afterwards, the narrator claims: "'O city,' I prayed, 'since the time is coming when I will no longer be able to communicate with you in my own language, allow me to rejoice to the end in the things that words correspond to when they break apart'" (41). The character shows a link with the city through language but residing in the space where words break, that is, in the fracture between language and the world where meaning is lost and silence emerges. If we interpret these lines as the rupture between the world and language, this extract mirrors one in *City of Glass*, the first novel of *The New York Trilogy*, in which one of its characters, Peter Stillman, Sr., explains to the protagonist, Daniel Quinn, his mission in New York and why he is picking up objects in the street:

> I have come to New York because it is the most forlorn of places, the most abject. The brokenness is everywhere, the disarray is universal. You have only

to open your eyes to see it. The broken people, broken things, broken thoughts. The whole city is a junk heap [Auster, *Trilogy* 78].

As a matter of fact, there is one more episode comparable to Auster's novel: in both cases, the narrator seems to be presenting an Apocalypse. In terms of what Blanchot comments in his essay "After the Fact,"

> the Apocalypse finally, the discovery of nothing other than universal ruin, which is completed with the fall of the last Tower, which is no doubt the Tower of Babel, while at the same time the owner is silently thrown outside (the being who has always assured himself of the meaning of the word "own"- apparently God, even though he is a beast), the narrator who has maintained the privilege of the ego, and the simple and marvelous girl, who probably knows everything, in the humblest kind of way [491].

As the passage describes, the protagonist arrives to a ruined tower which symbolizes the Tower of Babel. Apart from this, this tower has an owner and a girl who lives there and seems to be sick. The tower and the owner, who represents God, protect her; apparently it is the only safe place left. In this apocalyptic moment, there are two important elements: the room, which is a recurrent aspect throughout the whole story and basic for language and the process of writing creation to happen, and the tower, which stands for the Tower of Babel, ancient symbol of the language of the world. Compared with Auster's fiction, one of the central episodes of *City of Glass* deals with the Tower of Babel. Daniel Quinn, in his investigation and observation of Peter Stillman, Sr.'s movements, finds out that what the professor wants him to do is write the words "Tower of Babel" with his own footsteps. Here, the connections are explicit and it is not only the element that appears also in Auster's fiction, also its relation to language and what language means in the story as a perspective the American writer takes for his fiction.

Moreover, the narrator of Blanchot's story talks about a mirror inside the tower: "You could see through it to the outside and at the same time it reflected the things within" (47). Some lines later, the narrator continues: "By looking in the mirror I was better able to see how the rock piles had fallen into their present shapes-and how they preserved the memory of the past" (47). If the mirror also projects inside what is inside, there is a movement of multiplication that permits the phenomenon of duplicity to take place. In terms of Auster's fiction, more than the physical mirror, he uses the mirror effect as a recurrent resource to build up the action of his novels. Plots multiply and reflect inside the novel to create different fictional layers and stories within stories that end up having a repetitive effect, which is called the "mise en abyme" effect. This would justify the title of the first novel of the trilogy, *City of Glass*, as a space that reflects inside and projects outside stories and symbolizes the trilogy itself as a complete text that unites the three different novels.

The Invention of Solitude: *Paul Auster's Ars Poetica*

Before publishing these translations and even before writing the novels of the trilogy, Paul Auster published his first non-fiction book, *The Invention of Solitude*, in 1981. The book consists of two parts: "Portrait of an Invisible Man" and "The Book of Memory." The first part is dedicated to Auster's father, who had recently died when he began writing the book. It includes Auster's relationship with him as a son. The second part deals with the role of Auster as a father, and his relationship with his own son. Of course, these plots allow the American writer to talk about many other things and reflect about literature and his role as a writer. This book shows the influence Blanchot's theoretical principles on Auster. Particularly in this case, the American writer quotes and mentions Blanchot explicitly in this first work of non-fiction. In this sense, there are three different readings for this work: those parts in which Auster quotes Blanchot openly, those fragments in which Blanchot's theory permeates and all the extracts that contribute to the plot of the American writer's future novels.

Almost at the end of the section "Portrait of an Invisible Man," in the first part of the book, Auster quotes Blanchot:

> For the past two weeks these lines from Maurice Blanchot echoing in my head: "One thing must be understood: I have said nothing extraordinary or even surprising. What is extraordinary begins at the moment I stop. But I am no longer able to speak of it."
>
> To begin with death. To work my way back into life, and then, finally, to return to death.
>
> Or else: the vanity of trying to say anything about anyone [Auster, *Invention* 63].

This extract can be divided in two parts. The first statement quoted from Blanchot—"One thing must be understood: I have said nothing extraordinary or even surprising. What is extraordinary begins at the moment I stop. But I am no longer able to speak of it"—has two different interpretations. On the one hand, and on a superficial level, the French philosopher deals with his role as a writer and the effect his works could have on readers. On the other hand, he is also relating it to the work he produces and therefore to the act of writing. Again, as in his essay "After the Fact," the philosopher connects the process of writing and the writer with death. When he states, "But I am no longer able to speak of it" he takes the argument back to what Blanchot discussed in "After the Fact," asserting the connection between the writer and death. Indeed, Auster comments on the lines he quoted of Blanchot: "To begin with death. To work my way back into life, and then, finally to return to death."

In Auster's words, this would be in brief Blanchot's process of writing creation which includes the concepts of space, language, writer and death. Nevertheless, Auster does not leave his comment there. He adds to his reflection: "Or else: the vanity of trying to say anything about anyone." Here, the American writer is emphasizing the figure of the author and the arrogance that is required in order to sit in front of a piece of paper and write about something or someone. Actually, five pages later, Auster will focus his attention on Blanchot and the line that links the writer with death: "again Blanchot: 'But I am no longer able to speak of it'" (68). Essentially, this is the original condition of the author and, in a way, this could be the moment in which the process of creation is finished and everything is devoted to Blanchot's concept of invisibility.

In the text, there are other implicit allusions to the philosopher's principles. In the second part of the book titled "The Book of Memory" Auster describes in third person what the process of translation means to him. There is a fragment that summarizes the main topics of Blanchot's literary theory and remarkably, he describes all these points with a reflection about what is implied in being a translator, the role that connects him with the French philosopher. Auster claims:

> For most of his adult life, he has earned his living by translating the books of other writers. He sits at his desk reading the book in French and then picks up his pen and writes the same book in English. It is both the same book and

not the same book, and the strangeness of this activity has never failed to impress him. Every book is an image of solitude. It is a tangible object that one can pick up, put down, open and close, and its words represent many months, if not many years, of one man's solitude, so that with each word one reads in a book one might say to himself that he is confronting a particle of that solitude. A man sits alone in a room and writes. Whether the book speaks of loneliness or companionship, it is necessarily a product of solitude [136].

Auster uses the process of translation in order to illustrate solitude as the inexorable condition of the writer or translator and its projection in the product of translation, the book. However, the most notable part of the extract is when the narrator states, "A man sits alone in a room and writes. Whether the book speaks of loneliness or companionship, it is necessarily a product of solitude." Through this statement he is comparing the act of translation with the act of writing. Therefore, translator and writer carry out the same role in relation to the process of writing itself. And not only this, Auster is also asserting that the book is a product of solitude. Thus, he is presenting his own idea of solitude which can be defined as a condition essential for the act of writing which at the same time limits the individual as a writer. This definition is comparable to Blanchot's definition of essential solitude.

Throughout the book, Auster mixes real experiences with his thoughts about literature. Sometimes he discusses solitude in terms of his life experiences and others in relation to his role as a writer. To begin with, Auster introduces the idea of solitude through the figure of his father. The book starts with his father's death and this person is described as a very distant one who barely has contact with the narrator. In fact, Auster states that he writes this book in order to fill the space that his father never occupied as such. The title of the book is *The Invention of Solitude*, because Auster is trying to give shape to that solitude in which his father seemed to live. Also, this character is always described as an invisible person, sometimes because he acted as a blind man, or because he is treated like a ghost or a shadow- concepts that Blanchot uses to describe his theory of literature. For Auster he is the character who occupies solitude:

Like everything in his life, he saw me only through the mists of his solitude, as if at several removes from himself. The world was a distant place for him, I think, a place he was never truly able to enter, and out there in the distance, among all the shadows that flitted past him I was born, became his son, and grew up, as if I were just one more shadow, appearing and disappearing in a half-lit realm of his consciousness [24].

Although Auster does not make a clear reference to his father as writer or creator, he shares a lot of things with this figure. He is distanced from the world and seems to live in an inner space unknown by the outside world where the narrator, his son, is no more than a shadow. Yet, the concept of solitude is strongly linked to the idea of space; this is one of the reasons why Auster explains his father's solitude in connection to his situation in the world. With the purpose of connecting these two ideas, Auster continues to assert in the fragment dedicated to translation: "A. sits down in his own room to translate another man's book, and it is as though he were entering that man's solitude and making it his own" (136). Unavoidably solitude happens in the space of the room. To achieve that situation of isolation, Blanchot proposes a withdrawal to a room until the work is finished. Therefore, locked spaces become very important for the writing process and, in the future, for Auster's fiction. He starts introducing the idea of the space associated to the character of his father at the beginning of the book and, of course, in the section dedicated to him: "Portrait of an Invisible Man." The space in which Auster chooses to depict this condition is his father's house:

> The house became the metaphor of my father's life, the exact and faithful representation of his inner world. For although he kept the house tidy and preserved it more or less as it had been, it underwent a gradual and ineluctable process of disintegration [9].

There are two relevant expressions in this passage that can be connected to Blanchot's concept of space of literature: the "inner world" and the "process of disintegration." Although Auster's father is not a writer, the space he occupied all his life, according to Auster and in the context of the work, is a space of solitude. With him, the house suffers a process of disappearance similar to the one the writer undergoes in his own creative process. As a matter of fact, it is worthwhile to note that his father is treated as an invisible man. It is the portrait of an invisible man, image of his own process of disintegration. From this moment on, Auster will connect space with language, and will mention them together throughout the book. Intending to support the assumption that space and language have to be understood as inseparable and complementing features, he writes and interprets his father's life in relation to it, as in the following fragment:

Each time he goes out, he takes his thoughts with him, and during his absence the room gradually empties of his efforts to inhabit it. When he returns, he has to begin the process all over again, and that takes work, real spiritual work. [...] In the interim, in the void between the moment he opens the door and the moment he begins to reconquer the emptiness, his mind flails in a wordless panic. It is as if he were being forced to watch his own disappearance, as if, by crossing the threshold of this room, he were entering another dimension, taking up residence inside a black hole [77].

Through Blanchot's perspective, Auster is inventing a space of literature based on the locked space of his father's house, his solitude and his gradual disappearance. Indeed, the excerpt quoted above describes the spatial transformation suffered in a creative process. When Auster states, "by crossing the threshold of his room, he were entering another dimension, taking up residence inside a black hole," he is depicting the locked house as another world altered by his father's solitude and ruled by isolation.

The idea of the room is fundamental to Auster's intention to illustrate his space of invention and it will be in his future fiction.[8] In the excerpt quoted above, the room is described as an intimate space for the father where he projects his inner world that disappears the moment he leaves the room. What remains during his absence is an emptiness he has to reconquer once he comes back again. Auster describes this void as the reflection of his father's disappearance. Besides, crossing the threshold implies a projection of his father's inner world to an outside world that Auster describes some lines after as "an emanation of his mind" in which "he feels himself sliding through events, hovering like a ghost around his own presence" (78). Auster uses concepts similar to the ones used by the philosopher in order to explain and define the space of literature such as the room, the concept of absence, emptiness or void, and principally the projection of the inner world represented in the locked space of the room to the outside.

Together with this, Auster compares the concept of the room with two emblematic stories in the history of literature. One is the episode of Jonah and the whale, and the other is "Gepetto in the belly of the shark (the whale in the Disney version), and the story of how Pinocchio rescues him" (79). In order to give a definition of room, he uses these two stories and claims that a room is

a dream space, and its walls were like the skin of some second body around him, as if his own body had been transformed into a mind, a breathing instru-

33

ment of pure thought. This was the womb, the belly of the whale, the original site of the imagination [89].

The quotation explicitly relates the space of the room, which here is described as a "mind, a breathing instrument of pure thought" with "the original side of the imagination." Thus, the room is the material manifestation of the space of invention where the imagination and inner world of the writer is projected. Solitude is crucial in this whole process of creative transformation.

Apart from these two examples, Auster, like Blanchot, analyzes Hölderlin's text in order to formulate a theory of literature inscribed in the space of the room. Actually, the French philosopher openly uses Hölderlin's text with the purpose of creating and discussing his "ars poetica."[9] In Auster's case, Hölderlin intervenes as an example of how a room could bring Hölderlin back to life. Before this, Auster explains how Hölderlin's literary career started in a room during and after a mental breakdown. Having this in mind, Auster concludes,

> To withdraw into a room does not mean that one has been blinded. To be mad does not mean that one has been struck dumb. More than likely it is the room that restored Hölderlin to life, that gave him back whatever life it was left for him to live. As Jerome commented on the Book of Jonah, glossing the passage that tells of Jonah in the belly of the whale: "You will note that where you would think should be the end of Jonah, there was his safety" [100].

As described by Auster, the space of the room for Hölderlin becomes a healing and liberating place since the poet survives in the space of invention. Thus, in this case, Auster uses Hölderlin's example as a way to emphasize the literary aspect of the room in contrast with the absence and invisibility the room implied in his father's experience. Although both defining elements of the room seem contradictory, they complement and are necessary to make the imaginary space possible. Both aspects are fundamental in Maurice Blanchot's literary theory.

Yet, Auster proposes a new perspective. The second part of the book is titled "The Book of Memory." In it, the American writer bases the structure of his discourse and plot in a concept: memory. The definition of memory is progressively constructed along the second book of *The Invention of Solitude*, and Auster illustrates it again through his father's life and reflections about literature and the figure of the writer. The two concepts that are fundamental to defining Auster's understanding of memory can be explained through Blanchot's concepts of space and language. Auster's first introduction of the idea of memory in the text is connected to space:

> Memory as a place, as a building, as a sequence of columns, cornices, porticoes. The body inside the mind, as if we were moving around in there, going from one place to the next, and the sound of our footsteps as we walk, moving from one place to the next [82].

Some lines later, Auster states: "Memory as a room, as a body, as a skull that encloses the room in which a body sits" (82). According to Auster, memory is composed by one more element that can be inferred from his reflections on the topic. Once he has specified memory as a space, he asserts: "A world in which everything is double, in which the same thing always happens twice. Memory: the space in which a thing happens for the second time" (83). On the one hand, memory is the place that hosts an inward experience of the individual and, on the other hand, the space where something happens twice. We can compare this hypothesis with Auster's reflection about translation previously mentioned in the opening analysis of this book. He asserts, "For once solitude has been breached, once a solitude has been taken on by another, it is no longer solitude, but a kind of companionship. Even though there is only one man in the room, there are two" (136). This quotation takes into account the idea of the double in terms of Blanchot's definition and also the nature of repetition that is evident in the process of translation. Translation implies the rewriting of a text in which "a word becomes another word, a thing becomes another thing. In this way, he tells himself, it works in the same way that memory does" (136). In this way, language is part of the essence of memory in terms of the process of the repetition it suffers and the double nature it possesses.

Even though memory is described as a space of inwardness and solitude where repetition and infinite possibilities occur, it is also seen by Auster as "the only thing keeping him alive, and it was as though he wanted to hold off death for as long as possible in order to go on remembering" (118). In this context, Auster explains memory as a way of proving our lives in the present and how we have to leave our past behind with the aim of observing what surrounds us and existing only in our present. This is where the power of memory arises and "it is a way of living one's life so that nothing is ever lost" (138). Furthermore, he compares the act of remembering to the process of writing:

> A. has both a good memory and a bad memory. He has lost much, but he has also retained much. As he writes he feels that he is moving inward (through himself) and at the same time moving outward (toward the world) [139].

This extract echoes Blanchot's theory on the process of writing. Essentially, for Blanchot, writing is a double movement that starts in the solitude of the room and extends to the outside. It is evident that here, Auster is using Blanchot's steps in order to construct the space of memory: the essential solitude and the process of writing. In relation to this, he says: "The pen will never be able to move fast enough to write down every word discovered in the space of memory" (139).

The space of memory is the space of the past and the future but always in a multiplicative movement that opens the possibility of double stories, or stories that were lived in the past and now are recreated and lived in the present. In these terms, Auster asserts:

> Memory, therefore, not simply as the resurrection of one's private past, but an immersion in the past of others, which is to say: history-which one both participates in and is a witness to, is a part of and apart from. Everything, therefore, is present in his mind at once, as if each element were reflecting the light of all the others, and at the same time emitting its own unique and unquenchable radiance [139].

Memory becomes a space where infinite possibilities can take place and in this sense, this statement makes possible the association between memory and future. Auster explains this in the following sentence: "The reckless future, the mystery of what has not yet happened: this, too he learned, can be preserved in memory" (127). Here, Auster connects the act of speaking about the future with an abyss, which is a space that links what is said and what will happen. This abyss reminds us of the fracture that took place in discourse according to Blanchot and the space Auster calls memory:

> To speak of the future is to use a language that is forever ahead of itself, consigning things that have not yet happened to the past, to an "already" that is forever behind itself, and in this space between utterance and act, word after word, a chasm begins to open, and for one to contemplate such emptiness for any length of time is to grow dizzy, to feel oneself falling into the abyss [127].

Auster writes about utterance, the oral discourse that Blanchot translates as written text. Oral words can always become written words which, in the sequence of the writing process, open an empty space. In terms of Blanchot's theory, what remains there is silence, absence and invisibility. In a way, through his argument about memory and the future, Auster brings to his reflection the philosopher's idea of the space of literature. It also equalizes space of literature with space of memory and characterizes it with its immediate consequence: absence.

Blanchot's Theory of Literature

Maurice Blanchot can be considered a philosopher, a critic and a writer whose main task has been, as the critic Leslie Hill states, "to write within the interstices of the writings that, by chance or necessity, he encounters as a reader" (Hill 3). Blanchot's influences oscillate between Hegel's and Heiddeger's texts, as well as other poets and novelists that helped the French writer to justify his theoretical and philosophical reflections such as Nietzsche, Rilke, Mallarmé, Paulham, Kafka and Holderlin, among others. Hill asserts that Blanchot's discourse became more critical rather than being just an "exhaustive system of totalising concepts" (14) when he decided to answer the question that Mallarmé formulated in 1894—"Does something like literature exist?"—or, to be more precise, a question that he reformulates in Heideggerian terms as Hill explains:

> What are the implications for being of the statement that "something like Literature exists"? So when in 1955 *L'Espace Littéraire* came out, based on work published in *Critique* and the *Nouvelle Reveu Française* over the previous four years, it was apparent that Blanchot had at his disposal a critical idiom that, alongside its redoubtable philosophical sophistication, manifested, as the publisher's blurb put it, an experiential or experimental dimension entirely its own [14].

During the next fifteen years, Blanchot went on to publish his most important works in the *Nouvelle Reveu française*, essays and articles that were finally collected in different volumes that constitute the base for his theoretical corpus: *L'Espace littéraire* (1955), *Le Livre á venir* (1959), *L'Entretien infini* (1969), and *L'Amitié* (1971).

Maurice Blanchot's main work is *L'Espace littéraire* (1955), a book that presents the basic theoretical concepts of the philosopher. This volume is the starting point for other studies that elaborate and extend his literary theses but which always focus on answering the same question: "Does something like literature exist?" For Maurice Blanchot, the first step required for the formation of the literary space is what he calls "essential solitude." This concept opens Blanchot's book *L'Espace littéraire* (1955) as the beginning of the process of writing creation. Indeed, this idea will be reformulated in other volumes like *Faux Pas* (1941), *Le Livre á venire* (1959) and *L'Entretiene infini* (1969), referred to as the limit experience or the inner experience.

In the first section of the volume *The Space of Literature* (1955) titled "The Essential Solitude," Blanchot tries to define in detail what solitude means in the context of his study. He wonders what the expression "to be alone" means (Blanchot, *Space* 21) and concludes that "solitude as the world understands it is a hurt which requires no further comment here" (Blanchot, *Space* 21). Then, once this is outlined, he extends his definition to the figure of the artist and asserts:

> We do not intend to evoke the artist's solitude either—that which is said to be necessary to him for the practice of his art. When Rilke writes to the countess of Solms-Laubach (August 3, 1907), "For weeks, except for two short interruptions, I haven't pronounced a single word; my solitude has finally encircled me and I am inside my efforts just as the core is in the fruit," the solitude of which he speaks is not the essential solitude. It is concentration [21].

Blanchot explains that this kind of solitude is neither "the complacement of individualism" nor a "quest for singularity" (21), that is, it is the event that has to take place in order for the artist, who in this case is a writer, to start the process of creation, which is writing. Thus, the starting point for Maurice Blanchot's construction of a literary space is the solitude of the writer during the process of creation. This type of solitude differs from the one commonly known, the one that "leads us into melancholy reflections" (21). The writer, in order to be ready to write, or, more precisely, in order for the act of writing to be possible, has to be isolated in a particular way. Blanchot affirms:

> He who writes the work is set aside; he who has written it is dismissed. He who is dismissed, moreover, doesn't know it. This ignorance preserves him. It distracts him by authorizing him to persevere. The writer never knows whether the work is done. What he has finished in one book, he starts over or destroys in another [21].

One of the specific characteristics is that the nature of this state of solitude is infinite and so is the work that results from it. Indeed, Blanchot affirms "the work is infinite means (...) that the artist, though unable to finish it, can nevertheless make it the delimited site of an endless task whose incompleteness develops the mastery of the mind" (22).

Moreover, he concludes that the literary work "is neither finished nor unfinished: it is" (22). The writer and the reader belong to this solitude "which expresses nothing except the word *being*: the word which language shelters by hiding it, or causes to appear when language itself disappears into the silent void of the work" (22).

Blanchot includes the concept of absence to complete, clarify and extend his definition of essential solitude. Basically, absence is an idea intimately related with the nature of solitude and, in this case, Blanchot uses it as one of its most remarkable characteristics. Absence determines what happens in the space of solitude concerning the work, the participants, the writer and the reader, and the language used to form it. Of course, in Blanchot's words "this absence makes it impossible ever to declare the work finished or unfinished" (22). In this sense, absence signifies the limitless nature of the work of literature since, once it is finished, it is started over or destroyed entering in an infinite movement of creation. Here is where absence plays its part because always, what awaits at the beginning and remains at the end is nothing. Hence, absence is the essence of solitude, it is the beginning of the creative project, and it is at the end when the work is neither finished nor unfinished but simply exists. Blanchot concludes stating that the work is solitary but it does not remain incommunicable. Indeed, he asserts that "whoever reads it enters into the affirmation of the work's solitude, just as he who writes it belongs to the risk of this solitude" (22).

Evidently, as the main participants of the literary space, Blanchot explains the idea of the essential solitude in relation to the space created between the writer and the reader during the literary act. He starts by saying:

> There is a work only when, through it, and with the violence of a beginning which is proper to it, the word *being* is pronounced. This event occurs when the work becomes the intimacy between someone who writes it and someone who reads it [22–23].

However, the construction of his literary space does not exist separate from the idea of absence that governs "essential solitude" and which is central not only in the relation between the writer and the reader but also in the relation between the writer and his work. The writer exists in the absence of the essential solitude which governs the artistic result of his activities. In order to explain this, Blanchot affirms that "the writer who experiences this void believes only that the work is unfinished. [...] But what he wants to finish by himself remains interminable: it involves him in an illusory task" (Blanchot, *Space* 23). In other words, the writer never knows if his work is done since it is a work that starts over or is destroyed in another. Both theses conclude with absence as its immediate consequence, either in the interminable condition of the work or the inability of the writer to see the work finished. Actually, Blanchot explains the different forms in which the concept of absence can be expressed in the condition of essential solitude. In his opinion, "the writer, since he only finishes his work at the moment he dies, never knows of his work. One ought perhaps to turn this remark around. For isn't the writer dead as soon as the work exists?" (23). Here, Maurice Blanchot is introducing to his discussion the idea of the death of the author, a theme previously argued by other philosophers such as Roland Barthes or Michel Foucault.

The "illusory task" Blanchot makes reference to is the opening of a space of creation. This task is interminable and impossible for him to read. Indeed it would be only finished when the writer dies. The death of the author is always considered in terms of what Blanchot conceives of it: he stops writing, the reader stops reading and he is completely out of the work. The figure of the writer as the person who performs the activity of writing disappears, abandoning his space of creation. As mentioned before, this abandonment can only happen when the work exists, or as the French philosopher puts it, when the work "expresses nothing except the word *being*" (22). In relation to this, Blanchot explains:

> The writer's solitude, that condition which is the risk he runs, seems to come from his belonging, in the work, to what always precedes the work. Through him the work comes into being; it constitutes the resolute solidity of a beginning [24].

Thus, the French philosopher keeps mentioning a state that seems to be present throughout the space of solitude and which is in the origin of it, what he calls the beginning. The beginning exists before solitude and is present at the end of the process of writing when the writer abandons the work. If the work is interminable, and it exists essentially in a chain of repetition as Blanchot states, it is unavoidable that what remains both at the beginning and at the end of solitude is the beginning (24). It represents the original and final absence that exists in the creation of any piece of literary work. This process justifies Blanchot's affirmation about the nature of the work as interminable and incessant, a condition that belongs not only to the work but also, in extension, to the essence of the Blanchotian solitude. However, once he reaches this point in his analysis, he focuses on the process of writing, the figure of the writer and the concept of time that exists and governs the essential solitude.

In relation to the writer, Blanchot points out a fracture that exists between the writer and the world. In fact, he states, "to write is to break the bond that unites the word with myself" (26). In doing so, Blanchot is trying to present a total disconnection between the writer, the individual immersed in the essential solitude, and the world that surrounds him. In a way, it is a logical condition since part of the state of solitude implies a total isolation. Furthermore, this fracture happens through language, the tool with which the work is possible and, therefore, is an indispensable instrument for the literary work to exist and the ultimate aim of essential solitude. In this context, Blanchot concludes:

> To write is to break this bond. To write is, moreover, to withdraw language from the world, to detach it from what makes it a power according to which, when I speak, it is the world that declares itself, the clear light of day that develops through tasks undertaken, through action and time [26].

For Blanchot, language manifests in the act of speaking and he uses it in order to illustrate his theory about language. In this case, through language, the individual shows his connection with the world.[10]

Undoubtedly, this disconnection with the world affects the writer in relation to his identity. Blanchot begins by saying that the result of this fissure materializes in the fact that "the writer […] gives up saying 'I'" (26). With the intention of clarifying this affirmation, Maurice Blanchot quotes Kafka when he says that "he has entered into literature as soon as he can substitute 'He' for 'I'" (26). This statement can only be explained in the context of the Blanchotian essential solitude. If the work of literature can only happen in the space of the essential solitude and this space is governed by absence, it is certain that most of the activities that would take place there will also be supported by it. Furthermore, Blanchot adds:

> The writer belongs to a language which no one speaks, which is addressed to no one, which has no center, and which reveals nothing. He may believe he affirms himself in this language, but what he affirms is altogether deprived of self [26].

All the different features described by Blanchot on the fragment above explain the relationship of the writer with language and seem to have absence as the common meeting point. It is a language that encloses the writer more in his particular isolation and makes him different from the rest. In this sense, he leaves behind what he originally was—an individual connected to his world who spoke a known and ordinary language, to become someone else. And, this is the individual that has the exact characteristics to reach the essence of Blanchot's concept of solitude and become, inside this realm, a writer. The French philosopher explains that the figure of the writer is connected with the nature of the work and concludes: "Where he is, only being speaks-which means that language doesn't speak any more, but is. It devotes itself to the pure passivity of being" (27).

At this point, Blanchot introduces the idea of the imaginary to his reflection. The fracture is a new space where the separation between the individual and the world becomes a possibility for new images. In this case, Blanchot calls it new characters:

> If to write is to surrender to the interminable, the writer who consents to sustain writing's essence loses the power to say "I." And so he loses the power to make others say "I." Thus he can by no means live life to characters whose liberty would be guaranteed by his creative power. The notion of characters, as the traditional form of the novel, is only one of the compromises by which the writer, drawn out of himself by literature in search of its essence, tries to salvage his relations with the world and himself [27].

This is the origin of the space of literature. From the fracture emerges an imaginary space in which the distance between the writer and the world, between the individual and his "I" creates new characters that will occupy this new world. The same happens with the other instruments involved in the construction of this new place that is the case of language. This is the reason why Blanchot explains that "the writer belongs to a language which no one speaks, which is addressed to no one, which has no center, and which reveals nothing" (26).

In the whole process of the creative construction, essential solitude becomes a space. For Blanchot, the word space designates the activities and characters that undergo this process. In this context, in the moment solitude seems to be located in a space, or can be interpreted as a space, the French philosopher chooses a time for this scene. The time that limits this space is unavoidably regulated by absence, in the same way solitude is. Time becomes one more element present in the construction of solitude but totally dependent on the features that constitute this solitude. In relation to this, he affirms: "it is a time without negation, without decision, when here is nowhere as well, and each thing withdraws into its image while the 'I' that we are recognizes itself by sinking into the neutrality of a featureless third person" (30). As can be inferred from Blanchot's words, this definition of time is connected with writing, with the interminable nature of solitude and with the individual who dedicates this lapse of time to the act of writing. In this chain of connections, the French philosopher remarks: "The time of time's absence has no present, no presence. This 'no present' does not, however, refer back to a past" (30). If Blanchot understands this type of time as a concept which does not delimit the past, the present nor the future, it is because it is the time of absence, the period that controls absence. Therefore the conception of space under these different parameters differs from the one that is regulated by a time structured with the coordinates of the past, present and future. Up to this moment, Blanchot theorizes about an inner experience, that is, solitude or a voluntary state of the individual to withdraw and interact with the possibilities this situation offers. Of course, the French philosopher chooses some concrete actions that contribute to transform this solitude into an unusual one. Remarkably, the most significant activity that actually makes this kind of solitude different is the act of writing. Once these features are determined, he assumes that this state becomes a space. Thus, this is the moment in which this inner space, deserted and immersed in a profound absence that affects all its participants, starts to become what it was originally created for: a space of literature.

In order to justify "essential solitude" as the achievement of an imaginary space created by the writer through the process of writing, Blanchot introduces in his theory two new concepts: the idea of fascination and, as a consequence, the idea of the image. To start with, he defines this space of solitude as a fracture in which the image is possible. Indeed, Blanchot states: "for everything that is interior is deployed outwardly, takes the form of an image [...] the essence of the image is to be entirely outside, without intimacy and yet more inaccessible and more mysterious than the innermost thought" (Blanchot, *Book* 14). The image is a reproduction of what the writer is creating, and what he calls "fascination" rules this separation. The Blanchotian idea of fascination is the attraction that the literary image provokes when it is projected to the imaginary space. In these terms, it is the realization of the writing into metaphors and therefore, a transformation of the inner space into a literary space. In Blanchot's words: "what is given by contact at a distance is the image, and fascination is passion for the image" (Blanchot, *Space* 32). This imaginary or literary space is also called by Blanchot the "outside" since the whole inner experience of essential solitude is expressed in the act of writing and exteriorized in what he calls a "vertiginous separation" (31). He explains this with the following words: "Here the only space is its vertiginous separation. Here fascination regins" (31).

The last section of Blanchot's chapter "The Essential Solitude" in *The Space of Literature* is titled "Writing." Once he has defined essential solitude, he points out what its main function in the construction of the space of literature is and he states:

> To write is to enter into the affirmation of the solitude in which fascination threatens. It is to surrender to the risk of time's absence, where eternal starting over reigns. It is to pass from the first to the third person, so that what happens to me happens to no one, is anonymous insofar as it concerns me, repeats itself in an infinite dispersal. To write is to let fascination rule language. It is to stay in touch, through language, in language, with the absolute milieu where the thing becomes image again, where the image, instead of alluding to some particular feature, becomes an allusion to the featureless, and instead of a form drawn upon absence, becomes the formless presence of this absence, the opaque, empty opening onto that which is when there is no more world, when there is no world yet [33].

The act of writing for Blanchot is the final aim of this process of essential solitude. It occurs when the concept of image, which is a manifestation of Blanchot's idea of fascination, emerges in the text as fiction. Apart from this, Blanchot connects the project of writing with two other aspects that are essential for his theory of literature: the idea of language and the concept of the other. Both become tools indispensable for the construction of the space of literature. Language controls this new space governed by the concept of image and shows one of its principal features—"the thing becomes image again"—and, as he explains several lines afterwards, the image "becomes an allusion to the featureless, and instead of a form drawn upon absence, becomes the formless presence of this absence" (33).

At this point, Blanchot affirms two crucial ideas: firstly, he relates language with the image as its ultimate consequence, and secondly he connects both with the idea of absence. In this context, absence defines partially Blanchot's idea of language, a feature he explains and names as the death in language but always in relation to the language used to construct the imaginary space—that is, literary language. In other words, language and therefore literature are formed by a silence or void emerging at the end, not only in the resulting image that they construct, but also in every word expressed in any written text. This is the reason why Blanchot asserts that language is "the absolute milieu where the thing becomes image again," since language starts at the beginning of the process of writing and once the image is constructed, it manifests itself at the end. Thus, language creates a revolving or cyclical movement, as he calls it, "eternal starting over" or "infinital dispersal."

Additionally, Blanchot explains that to write is "to pass from the first to the third person, so that what happens to me happens to no one, is anonymous to me." Previously in the text, he mentions the idea of someone else witnessing the process of writing. He expresses it in the following terms: "When I am alone, I am not alone, but in this present, I am already returning to myself in the form of Someone. Someone is there, when I am alone" (31). This is his definition for the concept of the other. Here, this Someone can be explained as the transformation from the first person to an anonymous third person.[11]

In order to develop a theory of language, Maurice Blanchot takes Stephane Mallarmé's thoughts and experiences as a writer not only to define the behavior of language in the poem, and therefore in literature, but also to support and extract examples that will construct his ideology about language.[12] To begin with, he proposes an analysis of Mallarmé's idea of the word. According to the French poet, the word can be "crude or immediate on the one hand" and "essential on the other" (38–39), concepts he previously defined as "ordinary language" or "everyday use of language" and the "language of the poetic act." Essentially, the crude word is the immediate speech that individuals use in order to come into contact with objects and the world surrounding them. Also, it serves as a tool that gives the illusion of being immediate, even though it is not, as it represents something that is not present. The essential word is introduced as the opposite of the crude word. Indeed, it is also introduced as the language of thought and as the contrary to ordinary language. In relation to this, Blanchot states: "At these junctures he takes up and attributes to literature the language of thought, that silent movement which affirms in man his decision not to be, to separate himself from being, and, by making the separation real, to build the world" (41).[13]

The abstract concept of "silence" and therefore absence define Mallarmé's idea of "word." On this aspect, Blanchot explains: "Silent, therefore, because meaningless, crude language is an absence of words, a pure exchange where nothing is exchanged, where there is nothing real except the movement of exchange, which is nothing" (39). In this sense, this type of language is a language based on absence, and thus evokes the absence of everything. Likewise, Blanchot explains this language as the "language of the unreal" or the "fictive language which delivers us to fiction, comes from silence and returns to silence" (39). Although both discuss writing and the written word, they use speech or the spoken word as a previous step to reach the realm of the writing task. Blanchot states that crude speech gives us "the presence of things, 'represent' them" (39), whereas the essential word "moves them away, makes them disappear. It is always allusive; it suggests, evokes" (39). Also, he asserts that language resides not just in the act of speaking but in the act of thinking as well: "Thought is the pure word. In thought we must recognize the supreme language [...]. Since to think is to write without appurtenances or whispers, but with the immortal word still tacit, the world's diversity of idioms keeps anyone from proffering expressions which otherwise would be, in one stroke, the truth itself materially" (39).

For Blanchot, language "suppresses" the meaning of a word as a way to introduce the concept of negativity and therefore absence as the essential concepts defining language. In relation to this idea, he affirms: "Death alone allows me to grasp what I want to attain; it exits in words as the only way they can have meaning" (Blanchot, *Station Hill* 380). That which is attainable is literature, and death becomes the meaning of words and, by extension, the meaning of literature. In order to go on with the argumentation of his theory, he distinguishes between "common language" and "literary language." In this parallelism, death is the feature that marks the difference and turns "common language" into "literary language":

> To name cat is, if you like, to make it into a non-cat, a cat that has ceased to exist, has ceased to be a living cat, but this does not mean one is making it into a dog, or even a non-dog. That is the primary difference between com-

46

mon language and literary language. The first accepts that once the nonexistence of the cat has passed into the word, the cat itself comes to life again fully and certainly in the form of its idea [Blanchot, *Station Hill* 381].

As the excerpt above points out, it is death as Blanchot understands it that is the essence of literature. Due to the transformation of the word into the concept, literature emerges in the process of that change; Blanchot translates this idea into a death that governs the writer, the text, and finally the work.[14]

Apart from this, Blanchot states that once the writer tries to approach immediate language, "it changes its nature in his hand" (Blanchot, *Book* 207). He calls this the "leap of literature," a condition he also talks about in *The Space of Literature* and which implies the transformation of ordinary language in its disappearance when it is used into fiction. As a result, Blanchot calls this "the leap," an experience which is part of the act of writing, together with "the essence of writing" and "the snag in the experience" (Blanchot, *Space* 176). This experience can be considered the inspirational component of the process of writing. As Blanchot explains in *The Book to Come*:

A formidable transformation. What I possess through fiction, I possess only on condition of being it, and the being by which I approach it is what divests me of myself and of any being, just as it makes language no longer what speaks but what is; language becomes the idle profundity of being, the domain where the word becomes being but does not signify and does not reveal [Blanchot, *Book* 208].

In Mallarmé's words, literature has a central point that he defines as the moment when the complete realization of language coincides with its disappearance. All this can happen only due to the fact that the word implies the appearance of all that has disappeared, which becomes the imaginary, the incessant and the interminable. Also, the central point can be structured in two different moments: it represents the presence of the work but at the same time the total disappearance of it in the searching for the origin. Although this sounds extremely contradictory, according to Blanchot, this is the reason the work turns into literature. He writes:

In the poem, language is never real at any of the moments through which it passes, for in the poem language is affirmed in its totality. Yet in this totality, where it constitutes its own essence and where it is essential, it is also supremely unreal. It is the total realization of this unreality, an absolute fiction [Blanchot, *Space* 45].

Taking the poem as the supreme manifestation of language, once it arrives to its aesthetic essence it also approaches unreality in the same way that it exists in order to reach its non-existence. Certainly, it is this contradiction that makes the work of fiction come true, or as Blanchot says in the previous extract, "the total realization of its unreality." As Blanchot explains, the hidden moment of experience is where the work finally creates its own space and, in this sense, the space of literature starts to emerge. Furthermore, he defines this symbolic area as "the region anterior to the beginning where nothing is made of being, and in which nothing is accomplished" (Blanchot, *Space* 46).

Blanchot reaches the point in which language, in the process of writing, becomes a work of art. In this imaginary space, as he affirms "art seems to be the silence of the world, the silence or the neutralization of what is usual and immediate in the world, just as the image seems to be the absence of objects" (47). Despite this void in the culmination of language, fiction, or art, they can only exist within the essence of absence. That being so, Blanchot describes the essence of writing from this point of view:

> Writing never consists in perfecting the language in use, rendering it purer. Writing begins only when it is the approach to that point where nothing reveals itself, where, at the heart of dissimulation, speaking is still but the shadow of speech, a language of the imaginary, the one nobody speaks, the murmur of the incessant and interminable which one has to silence if one wants, at last, to be heard [48].

In *The Book to Come*, Blanchot gives "the central point" a different name, one that better corresponds to its meaning. For him it becomes "the degree zero of writing": the maximum stage of absence that language can reach in the movement of writing. As he explains, it is that degree through which literature disappears. He writes:

> To write without "writing," to bring literature to that point of absence where it disappears, where we no longer have to dread its secrets, which are lies, that is "the degree zero of writing," the neutrality that every writer seeks, deliberately or without realizing it, and which leads some of them to silence.[15] [Blanchot, *Book* 207].

In order to discuss the topic of writing, Blanchot finds necessary to link it with the idea of the writer and with the idea of death. Throughout *The Space of Literature*, the idea of solitude is the threshold and the act of writing is its most immediate consequence which stands as a bridge to the space of literature. Here, the figure of the writer and his role in the process of creation is crucial together with language and how it affects the role of the writer and the construction of the space of literature as the culmination of the whole process. Part of Blanchot's theory is also based on the work of Franz Kafka (1883–1924), a contribution that helped Blanchot formulate and structure his literary principles.

First of all, he starts with Kafka's following statement: "I do not separate myself from men in order to live in peace, but in order to be able to die in peace" (Blanchot, *Space* 93). Here, Kafka mixes two concepts already familiar in Blanchot's ideology: isolation or solitude and death. To begin with, solitude is imposed by the impact of the work; that is, the need for solitude is "imposed upon him by his work" (93). In this context, the activity mentioned as "work" is writing. In order to continue with his argument, Blanchot explains that Kafka interprets solitude as a way to break with the world, an idea Blanchot analyzes previously in his work. At this point of the study, both Blanchot and Kafka express that it is fundamental for the writer to distance and isolate himself from the world that surrounds him in order to produce any kind of writing, or work, as Kafka calls it. However, Kafka introduces one new idea in relation to writing when he states, "I do not hide from men because I want to live peacefully, but because I want to perish peacefully" (93). Death, as the shadow of literature, plays a very important role in the act of writing and in the figure of the writer. In Blanchot's words, death here "is represented as the wages of art" and "it is the aim and justification of writing" (93).[16]

Thus what the individual, as creator of a piece of writing confronts is the origin of the literary piece. This idea becomes the reason why Blanchot concludes "whenever thought is caught in a circle" as it is in this case since it has reached "the profundity of experience," "this is because it has touched upon something original" (93). Some lines after this, Blanchot states that there is no possibility of movement except to return. In this sense, he insists that in order to reach this origin, it is necessary to disregard, from Kafka's words, "content" and "peacefully." Doing so, Blanchot is able to formulate the following statement based on Kafka's thoughts: "the writer, then, is one who writes in order to be able to die, and he is one whose power to write comes from an anticipated relation with death" (93). Clearly, there is a contradiction in this formula. On the one side, the process of writing implies a progressive

49

erasure of those coming into contact with language, in this case the writer, achieving at the end a literary death. In this respect, Bruns states, according to Blanchot in relation to his analysis of Kafka's work, "Writing is an act of dying" and "the work of art dying produces, or leaves behind, as if death were merely the trace of dying, not the completion of this process but simply the presence of everything finished" (Bruns 67). Yet, at the same time and according to what Kafka asserts, the only way to reach the work is through having previous contact with death. Indeed, Kafka summarizes this dilemma by saying: "Write to be able to die-Die to be able to write" (Blanchot, *Space* 94), an infinite recurrence that always comes back to the origin to die and remarks on the "radical reversal" that death signifies for Blanchot.

It is interesting how Blanchot connects what he calls the "leap" in death with the concept of inspiration. Instead of talking about death as the starting point or the origin for the artistic project, he now mentions the act of writing moved by inspiration as the precise step needed in order to arrive in the space of creation. Indeed, Blanchot states that: "one writes only if one reaches that instant which nevertheless one can only approach in the space opened by the movement of writing" (Blanchot, *Space* 176). In relation to this, Blanchot affirms:

> We come back here to what Kafka, at least in the sentences we ascribed to him, seemed to seek to express: I write to die, to give death its essential possibility, through which it is essentially death, source of invisibility; but at the same time, I cannot write unless death writes in me, makes of me the void where the impersonal is affirmed [149].

In a subsequent work, Blanchot reflects upon the idea of disappearance of the author in Mallarmé's critique. In *The Book to Come* Blanchot quotes Mallarmé in order to formulate and support his thesis about the disappearance of the author in the work of literature: "the work implies the elocutory disappearance of the poet, who cedes the initiative to words, set in motion by the clash of their inequality" (Blanchot 228). Following Mallarmé's statement, Blanchot explains the author's vanishing experience as something associated with language. Thus, he concludes that "the poet, by the fact that he speaks poetically, disappears into this language and becomes the very disappearance that is accomplished in language, the only initiator and principle: the source" (Blanchot, *Book* 229). Still, in this case, the French philosopher remarks on the importance of the existence of the author in a first stage of creation and how, paradoxically, the situation becomes reversed and causes the author's disappearance to become an essential component of the process of writing:

> The book is without author because it is written from the eloquent disappearance of the author. It needs the writer, insofar as the writer is absence and place of absence. The book is book when it does not refer back to someone who made it, as unstained by his name and free of his existence as it is of the actual intention of the one who reads it [Blanchot, *Book* 229].[17]

The presence of death as the essential component of experience,[18] that is the search for the origin of the work and its impossibility, also plays an important role in the ambiguity or double nature of the concept. In Blanchot's words, the writer is only able to write and start a work of literature if he has experienced death previously. Blanchot writes that "the writer, then, is one who writes in order to be able to die, and he is one whose power to write comes from an anticipated relation with death" (Blanchot, *Space* 93). Although this contradiction might be considered a feature that blocks the creative process of writing, it actually justifies the parallelism and identification between experience and origin. Again, as Blanchot asserts, Kafka summarizes this opposition in a very simple way: "write to be able to die-Die to be able to write" (94). Additionally, Blanchot supports this quotation with a contrary thesis: "To write in order not to die, to entrust oneself to the survival of the work: this motive is apparently what keeps the artist at his task" (94). Nevertheless, it is in the survival of the work where death resides in the sense that the accomplishment of the work brings death unfailingly.

Blanchot's analysis widens his perspective when his conception of death is transferred to the idea of space. He explains that death is contemporary to us as an event that we are all aware will take place at some point in our lives. Thus death, as he writes, "exists not only, then, at the moment of death; at all times" (Blanchot, *Space* 133). In any case, the individual is incapable of looking at it or, as Blanchot says, he is turned away from it because as a human being, he is limited by the constraints of everyday life. Individuals are limited by time and space, and these are the most important characteristics that define the space occupied by life. Rather than conceiving life and death as opposite concepts, Maurice Blanchot understands them both as complementary sides that affect and limit the existence of the individual. Indeed, he defines the other side as "the side which is not turned toward us, nor do we shed light upon it" (133). Bearing this in mind, Blanchot proposes a way in which the individual would be able to destroy his limits and look at the other side that encompasses death through artistic representation. In order to grasp any of the things we are turned away from, it is necessary to represent them by transforming them into an object or objective reality that at the same time makes the individual feel he owns it. Again, Blanchot is once more establishing a connection between death and literature since what he defines as the space of death would be imagined or brought to objective reality by the individual through representation in the same way he represents the world through language. Thus, there is an intersection between these two realms in the sense both are in some way or another represented by the individual's consciousness.

In the same way that he uses Kafka's literature in order to define his own idea of the writer, this time Blanchot refers to Rilke's texts as a way to outline his theory about space and concretely how this theory relates to death. In relation to Rilke, Blanchot starts by stating that the only way the individual has to arrive at the other side is by transforming the way in which he can access it. According to him, Rilke proposes consciousness as the door to enter the other side. In this way, it is consciousness that becomes the state through which the individual is able to construct a representation of that side that remains behind the objective perception of reality. In relation to this proposal, Blanchot concludes that there are two obstacles that impede the entrance to the other side: the exterior world and the inner side of the individual. In this context, Blanchot's analysis of space and death is comparable to the construction of his theory of the fictional space. Here, Blanchot suggests a combination of the two sides as obstacles in the individual's quest to reach the other side. Blanchot begins by writing about a first obstacle, which he calls a "bad extension," and refers to the basic limitations of the individual in terms of time and space. Following this idea, he presents a second obstacle: "bad interiority," in which the individual is already interpreting his exterior world from his consciousness. He concludes: "space is at once intimacy and exteriority" (136); this is the beginning of the construction of a space of fiction. Blanchot completes his definition of space by adding that this space "is scanned" and "intimated" but "dissipates and remains according to the various expressive forms of the written work" (136). Also, he affirms here that "story is replaced by hypothesis" and time, as we conceive ordinary time, is absolutely out of it (Blanchot, *Book* 239).

However, Rilke believes in a last chance to enter the inner space. Instead of turning our gaze towards the objective reality "where we dwell in the security of stable forms and separate existence," he proposes to look for a deep intimacy "toward the most interior and the most invisible, where we are no longer anxious to do and act, but free of ourselves and of real things and of phantoms of things" (Blanchot, *Space* 138). Blanchot, commenting on Rilke, makes reference to the fact that it is still possible to go one step further into that "world of representations which is only the double of objects" which is created by language, and attain one more layer of representation. Hence, the origin of space implies the transgression of different layers of representation that at an initial level offer a fake representation of the world, and in a deeper movement, open a conceptual layer in which invisibility and intimacy stand for representation, becoming the pillars of a new space. In fact, Blanchot previously mentions the idea of the conception of the book as a work that repeats itself in an infinite movement inside the same space:

> The book that is the Book is one book among others. It is a numerous book, multiplied in itself by a movement unique to it, in which diversity, in accordance with the various depths and space where it develops, is necessarily perfected. The necessary book is subtracted from chance. Escaping chance by its structure and its delimitation, it accomplishes the essence of language, which uses things by transforming them into their absence and by opening this absence to the rhythmic becoming that is the pure movement of relationships [Blanchot, *Book* 226].

Also, Blanchot makes reference to the multiplicity of the book in *The Infinite Conversation*, when he affirms that "the fact that the book is always undoing itself (dis-arranging itself) still only leads to another book or to a possibility other than the book, not to the absence of the book" (430). In this sense, Blanchot supports the existence of several layers that can stand for different books.

The immediate consequence of this transgression of different perceptive layers is the achievement of what Rilke calls the "heart's intimacy" (Blanchot, *Space* 138) that, at the same time, he defines as an imaginary space. Here, in this stage, consciousness looks for unconsciousness as its solution that is only possible, as Rilke explains, due to a transformation at the level of signification. At this level, the individual becomes "as fully conscious as possible of our existence" (138) since the realm he reaches at this stage of perception and reproduction of reality, what we understand as the immediate world, the "here" and "now," is not anymore limited by time but is instead measured by what Rilke describes as "superior significances" (139). In relation to this, Blanchot explains that the expression "superior significances" provides evidence for the existence of an interiority that is totally free of "everything that makes it a substitute for the objective real which we call the world" (139), and remains in what can be considered a higher level in the sense that the concepts that comprise this inner space seem to be those which are its source. Thus, the foundations of the imaginary space, or in other words, of the most interior spaces, have been reached. Blanchot clarifies that it is not the bad consciousness he mentioned before in relation to Rilke's reflections, it is a consciousness more profound that has the power to transcend to that point in which consciousness breaks to the outside. Through Rilke's words, the imaginary space exists at that point in which signification or the concept itself rules any perception.

The next step in this progressive transgression of different layers of consciousness and representation opens to the space of the outside. Blanchot considers this a change of the visible into the invisible: "This transformation of the visible into the invisible and of the invisible into the always more invisible takes place where the fact of being unrevealed does not express a simple privation, but access to the other side" (139–140). This transformation is the moment in which a text, governed by the crude word, enters the realm of the essential word and turns everything into the most inner invisibility. Accordingly, it is possible to connect the invisibility of the concept left by interiorization and the idea of death as a literary death in terms of what Blanchot explains since what remains is a void which represents the inner space. Certainly, several lines after, Blanchot asserts:

> Thus we see that conversion—the movement toward the most interior, a work in which we transform ourselves as we transform everything—has something to do with our end, and that this transformation, this fruition of the visible in the invisible for which we are responsible, is the very task of dying, which has until now been so difficult for us to recognize [141].

The most important element in this transformation to the invisible is language. Here, Blanchot distinguishes between two different spaces, the objective one and the imaginary. On the one hand, in the objective space represented by the world, he affirms "things are *transformed* into objects in order to be grasped" (141). These things occupy a limited and divisible space. On the other hand, Blanchot proposes an imaginary space in which "things are *transformed* into that which cannot be grasped" (141). In opposition to the objective reality, imaginary space is released from any limitation. Thus Blanchot adds that things "are not in our possession but are the movement of dispossession which releases us both from them and from ourselves" (141). In order to clarify the link between the concept of death, the inner space, and the concept of language, Blanchot utilizes one of Rilke's ideas, writing that the interior space "translates things" (141). Blanchot infers from one of Rilke's last poems that "it makes them pass from one language to another, from the foreign, exterior language into a language which is altogether interior and which is even the interior of language, where language names in silence and by silence, and makes of the name a silent reality" (141).

Blanchot concludes that if we consider the idea that the interior space translates things, we can assume that "the essential translator is the poet" (141); and thus, once all the different components (interiority, death and language) are connected, "this space is the poem's space, where no longer is anything present, where in the midst of absence everything speaks" (141). Hence, if the translator is the poet and the space is the poem, Blanchot states that the conversion from the visible to the invisible takes place in the word. That is to say, "to speak is essentially to transform the visible into the invisible; it is to enter a space which is not divisible, an intimacy which, however, exists outside oneself" (142). Likewise, Blanchot calls this open space the "Orphic space" (142), to which the writer cannot penetrate unless he disappears in it. Concretely, Blanchot claims that the writer attains this place "only when he is united with the intimacy of the breach that makes him a mouth unheard, just as it makes him who hears into the weight of silence" (142). Therefore, after the long process of the transformation, that is, the act of writing creation and its different phases, it is only at the end when the writer reaches this state in which he, as creator, dissolves into the silence left by the words he has written. In this sense, the silence brings about an open space that takes the writer to an original silence that existed before any word could have been created: when the work was a blank piece of paper. And again, coming back to the beginning, the writer, as Blanchot asserts, becomes the essential translator.

2

The Gaze of Orpheus
A Theory of Inspiration

One of the most significant contributions of Blanchot's process of creation and theory of literature is his thesis of the idea of inspiration. Blanchot takes as a central pillar for his definition of inspiration the Greek myth of Orpheus and Eurydice and how the denouement of the story, and therefore the ultimate loss suffered by Orpheus, can be interpreted as an illustration of the connection between the writer and his work, moreover, as the impulse or leap that makes literature possible. Apart from this, Blanchot links the theory of inspiration with the idea of the other, a concept that emerges from the process of inspiration. Although the concept of the other is also mentioned by Blanchot as an unavoidable consequence in the initiation of writing, it is better understood in the context of inspiration, which is also a necessary element in the process of writing. There are some of Auster's works such as *Ghosts* (1986), *The Music of Chance* (1990) or *Mr. Vertigo* (1994) that deal with the topic of inspiration exclusively and focus all the fictional discourse on that thesis.

Timothy Clark in his work *The Theory of Inspiration* (1997) presents an analysis of Blanchot's theory of inspiration. In it, he affirms that Blanchot's work seems to put an end to the romantic idea of inspiration as a human power (Clark 239) and takes "these Romantic and modernist criteria of value to a radical extreme at which they undergo a qualitative transformation, one which justifies the increased recognition of Blanchot's place in the genealogy of deconstruction" (239). Clark concludes that Blanchot's innovation resides in how this transformation takes place since it is focused on the "crisis of subjectivity undergone by the writer in the process of writing" (239). Yet, Clark begins his interpretation by stating that one of the differences established by Blanchot is the fact that for him inspiration comes from outside:

> By definition inspiration finds its provenance outside or beyond the consciousness of the writer; in Blanchot the outside from which inspiration comes is, counterintuitively, both the emerging work itself and, literally, nowhere. Inspiration forms a complex and contradictory passion, one that does not belong to the writer, but takes possession from out of nothing [238].

Clark describes in a very concrete way the two distinct sides from which inspiration comes, as Blanchot understands it. The French philosopher starts Chapter V of his work *The Space of Literature* titled "Inspiration" by asserting, "Whoever devotes himself to the work is drawn by it toward the point where it undergoes impossibility" (Blanchot, *Space* 163). This is related to what Clark has called the "crisis of subjectivity undergone by the writer in the process of writing" since the writer is drawn by the work to a point in which, according to Blanchot, he reaches impossibility. Blanchot demands from the writer a total surrender to the work of art; this implies leaving his self and his connection to the world behind. Also, this "crisis of subjectivity" is repeated and is the main theme of most of Auster's novels.

When Blanchot refers to impossibility, he claims that this episode is what he calls a nocturnal experience or "the very experience of night" (163). Actually, night is parallel to his idea of impossibility in the sense that for him night is that place where everything has disappeared and absence approaches (163). Then, Blanchot compares impossibility with the idea of night because it is the instant in which everything disappears but where "everything [that] has disappeared" appears. In this sense, the moment the writer reaches impossibility, he gets to the realm where everything that disappears takes its shape. Blanchot elaborates in the following terms: "here the sleeper does not know he sleeps, and he who dies goes to meet real dying. Here language completes and fulfills itself in the silent profundity which vouches for it as its meaning" (163). In this context, Blanchot calls this night *the other night* in order to distinguish it from what he calls the night, that place which "is inaccessible because to have access to it is to accede to the outside, to remain outside the night and to lose forever the possibility of emerging from it" (164). Furthermore, he states, "*In* the night one can die; we reach oblivion. But this *other* night is the death no one dies, the forgetfulness which gets forgotten. In the heart of oblivion it is memory without rest" (164). Therefore, the realm of impossibility is what Blanchot calls *the other night*, in which disappearance appears, where impossibility emerges and, consequently, where the writer has to be in order to let the literary space exist. Indeed, he asserts: "here the invisible is what one cannot cease to see; it is the incessant making itself seen" (163). If here the invisible and the incessant become visible and this is the realm where "language completes and fulfills itself in the silent profundity which vouches for it as its meaning," evidently Blanchot is describing the space opened by writing and accordingly the only way the writer can get here is through it.

One of the ideas that Maurice Blanchot develops about the night is the act of sleeping compared with the act of dying. In Blanchot's words, the act of dying in the literary context implies the freedom of man from being and permits the individual to "move beyond myself toward the world of others" (165). This movement refers to what Blanchot proposes when he talks about the writer and the transformation that takes place in him when he is immersed in the process of creation. Here, it is possible to take Blanchot's words again when he claims that the writer, in the solitude of the work, returns to himself in the form of someone, a figure he finally defines as an "other"[1] (31). Blanchot concludes that once the individual is freed from his being, what remains is nothingness and it is this nothingness that becomes his power since the individual is able not to be (164). Another time, this last argument connects with Blanchot's idea of the condition of the writer. In other words, the writer reaches this moment of absence when he embraces this nothingness Blanchot is referring to, and accordingly is totally immersed in a state of inspiration.

Concepts like night or death still belong for Blanchot to that realm in which the possibility of opening what he calls the "other night" exists and the appearance of someone else he considers "the other" becomes possible. In order to explain these two different events, Maurice Blanchot establishes a kind of dialectical relation between the concepts of night and day. Interpreted as two different spaces, Blanchot explains that these two moments are interrelated in a co-dependent connection in which there is no way one exists without the other. Furthermore, Blanchot's thesis proposes the idea of night as the inner part of day, as that instant of the existence of day that it is yearning to reach. In relation to this, Blanchot states:

Night is what day wants not just to dissolve, but appropriate: night is thus the essential, which must not be destroyed but conserved, and welcomed not as a limit but for itself. Night must pass into day. Night becoming day makes the light richer and gives to clarity's superficial sparkle a deep inner radiance. Then day is the whole of the day and the night, the great promise of the dialect [167].

In this sense, night can be considered to be the essential part of day and, from the beginning of its existence, day is yearning to reach it, an instant Blanchot also compares to the moment of death. Indeed, Blanchot concludes, "Only the day can feel passion for the night. It is only in the day that death can be desired, planned, decided upon—reached" (168). Thus, Blanchot is again proposing an infinite cyclical movement in which day longs for night and night transforms into day; it is only in the moment the day reaches the night when freedom occurs. However, this cyclical movement implies a transformation so night always comes back to day but always in a different state. This is what Blanchot calls "the other night" in contrast with the "first night." According to the French critic, "In the first night it seems that we will go—by going further ahead—toward something essential. And this is correct, to the extent that the first night still belongs to the world and, through the world, to day's truth" (168). Nevertheless, he presents another aspect of the night he calls the "other night" and which is a result of its contact with the essence of day. So, "the *other* night is revealed as love that breaks all ties, that wants the end and union with the abyss" (68). It is fundamental to reach the instant of the night in order to experience inspiration; this is the reason why the individual reaches what Blanchot calls "night" through the total isolation and withdrawal of the individual writer in the locked space of the room.[2] Here, the character reaches the "other night" or the moment of inspiration that opens the literary space. At the same time, once the 'impersonal affirmation emerges,' it is possible to refer back to Blanchot's idea of the "other" or the *autrui*.

Essentially, this moment of inspiration is considered by the French critic to be a limit or inner experience. Among all the several definitions he gives for this state, he asserts that "the limit-experience is the response that man encounters when he has decided to put himself radically in question" (Blanchot, *Conversation* 203), but more importantly he concludes that "interior experience is the manner in which the radical negation that no longer has anything to negate *is affirmed* [...]. It affirms nothing, reveals nothing, communicates nothing. Then one might be content to say that the affirmation is this 'nothing' communicated" (208); thus, the limit-experience offers affirmation for the first time this experience "represents something *like* a new origin" (208–209). According to Timothy Clark, for Blanchot literary inspiration is a limit experience because it is "an experience of insecurity that enacts a crisis in the relation to beings as a whole"[3] (Clark 240).

If the limit-experience is the affirmation of "nothing," the individual seeks for it through what Blanchot calls the plural speech. In this way, Blanchot justifies the use of language to express inspiration and opens not only the other side but also lets the other or *autrui* emerge. In this context, Maurice Blanchot presents a speech in which he involves two different entities or voices that establish a non-dialectical speech but who say "the same thing, for they neither discuss nor speak of subjects able to be approached in diverse ways" (Blanchot, *Conversation* 215). Here, the French philosopher theorizes about these two speakers who share the space of the plural speech and concludes that one of them represents the other or *autrui*, which is the result of this non-dialectical speech:

> One could say of these two speaking men that one of them is necessarily the obscure "Other" that is *Autrui*. And who is Autrui? The unknown, the stranger, foreign to all that is either visible or non-visible, and who comes to "me" as speech when speaking is no longer seeing. One of the two is the Other: the one who, in the greatest human simplicity, is always close to that which cannot be close to "me": close to death, close to the night. But who is me? Where is the Other? The self is sure, the Other is not-unsituated, unsituatable, nevertheless each time speaking and in this speech more Other than all that is other. Plural speech would be this unique speech where what is said one time by "me" is repeated another time by 'Autrui" and thus given back to its Difference [215–216].

The Gaze of Orpheus

One of the most remarkable contributions to the theory of inspiration is Maurice Blanchot's analysis and reflection about the Greek myth of Orpheus. With it, Blanchot presents an example of how the instant of inspiration takes place—in other words, Blanchot proposes a way of explaining how what he considers to be the realm of night opens and how this instant takes place through art: "When Orpheus descends toward Eurydice, art is the power by which night opens" (Blanchot, *Space* 171). Desperate for the loss of his wife Eurydice, Orpheus, the musician of Olympus, becomes one of the few Greek characters allowed to descend into the underworld. His aim is to take her back to the world of the living and, while he tries, he transgresses the unique condition imposed by the Gods to achieve his aim: he looks back at Eurydice while they are ascending from Hades. These two moments become extremely relevant in support of Blanchot's thesis. The catabasis, and especially the encounter with Eurydice, justifies what Blanchot considers the opening of the night: "she is the profoundly obscure point toward which art and desire, death and night, seem to tend. She is the instant when the essence of night approaches as the *other* night" (171).

Through Eurydice and her significance in the Greek literary history, the French philosopher explains that instant in which the imaginary space of literature opens. Therefore it is the precise moment in which Orpheus turns to see his wife again when the fictional and poetic space emerges. In this respect, Blanchot affirms that Orpheus's work "is to bring it back to the light of day and to give it form, shape, and reality in the day," however, and he continues "Orpheus is capable of everything, except of looking this point in the face, except of looking at the center of night in the night"[4] (171).

Although the Greek myth presents Orpheus as the eternal lover capable of doing anything to recuperate his wife, Blanchot understands this act of love in literary terms as the attempt to transform all those elements that shape the real referent of the author and bring them back in a new space and in the form of an image. Orpheus is mainly bringing light out of darkness; it is the fact of transforming one thing into the other—that is, from the movement of negation appropriate of death into a movement of truth—that only takes place in the realm of day (Bruns 70).[5] What Orpheus would be bringing back from the world of the living is something different, not his wife, someone else, an *autrui* that essentially belongs to the realm Blanchot calls the other night which is the new fictional space consequence of this instant of inspiration. Then, one of the most significant details that connects Eurydice with literature in terms of Blanchot's theory of literature is her union with death and how that transforms her into a shady and ghostly figure that is being dragged to life again. Indeed, Bruns asserts that Orpheus's desire is to have her as the reflection of the essence of night, as an image of darkness: "It is not her beauty that he desires but Eurydice herself, Eurydice in darkness, *as* darkness, the essence of the night (the other night): Eurydice the foreign and inaccessible (*autrui*)" (Bruns 70).

In relation to this, Eurydice's contact with death makes her comparable to Blanchot's idea of language and how it is linked to death in literary terms. Together with this, and in order to explain Eurydice's nature, Blanchot introduces another remarkable event not only for the plot of the myth but also for the argumentation of his thesis. Orpheus's story is based on his failure—that is to say, his uncontrollable desire and impatience make him turn back and look at his wife before they both reach the world of the living. Blanchot comments on this saying: "When he looks back, the essence of night is revealed as the inessential. Thus, he betrays the work, and Eurydice, and the night" (Blanchot, *Space* 172). He also states that Orpheus cannot look this point in the face, that is, he cannot look at her since she is the center of night in the night: "he can descend toward it; he can and this is still stronger an ability—draw it to him and lead it with him upward, but only by turning away from it. This turning away is the only way it can be approached" (171). However, Blanchot concludes that Orpheus's failure is indispensable in order for the imaginary, or what he calls nocturnal space, to be opened. Whereas from the point of view of the myth it is a total tragedy that leaves its protagonist in agony and despair, for Blanchot, and in literary terms, Orpheus's failure is a success. Blanchot formulates it in the following way:

> But not to turn toward Eurydice would be no less untrue. Not to look would be infidelity to the measureless, imprudent force of his movement, which does not want Eurydice in her daytime truth and her everyday appeal, but wants her in her nocturnal obscurity, in her distance, with her closed body and sealed face–wants to see her not when she is visible, but when she is invisible, and not as the intimacy of a familiar life, but as the foreignness of what excludes all intimacy, and wants, not to make her live, but to have living in her the plenitude of her death [172].

In this context, Eurydice becomes an image of the night, someone who belongs to the world of the dead. In relation to this, Timothy Clark comments that the poetic space is that in which contradictions are not impossible but are not solved either and claims, "the literary is an experience of impossibility, the unpredictable result of contradictory facts almost entirely beyond authorial control. Yet these same factors are also the condition for the emergence of the work as something radically novel" (245). This would explain the necessity of Orpheus's failure and the impossibility of his deed. Thus, it is this contradiction that makes the poetic space emerge and makes literature possible. In the same line of thought, Leslie Hill in his work *Blanchot: Extreme Contemporary* (1997) explains this contradiction with two opposite concepts, patience and impatience, based on Blanchot's statement: "impatience must be the core of profound patience" (Blanchot, *Space* 176). In Hill's words, "patience is impatience deferred" and, therefore, both seem to work as dialectical contraries in which synthesis or unification is literally impossible (20). In this way, Hill finally concludes "Orpheus's sacrifice of Eurydice does not lead therefore to the work, but to the sacrifice of the work, and to the affirmation of the impossibility of the work as the secret of its origin" (120).

Orpheus's error condemns Eurydice to remain as a shadowy image, an appearance, as Blanchot mentions: "he saw her invisible, he touched her intact, in her shadowy absence, in that veiled presence which did not hide her absence, which was the presence of her infinite absence" (Blanchot, *Space* 172). It is in this instant when art happens, or when the imaginary space emerges. As Timothy Clark remarks, in *The Infinite Conversation* Blanchot expresses the poetic space as a turn, as a "place of dispersion, disarranging and disarranging itself, dispersing and dispersing itself beyond all measure" (23), and Clark comments that this "turning" in language and in speech is a "movement, always present in language, of errancy, of signifying without form" (Clark 244). Language, in this poetic space, imposes a silence and therefore the writer remains in a constant contradiction that Blanchot expresses in this "turning," that "at the moment when it is about to emerge, makes the work pitch strangely. This is a work in which as its always decentered center, holds sway: the absence of work" (Blanchot, *Conversation* 32). With this reflection, Blanchot expresses the same concept as the figure of Eurydice, the writer goes towards an unavoidable absence produced by speech that in some way is represented by the ghostly image of Eurydice. Blanchot asserts that "the absence of work in which discourse ceases so that, outside speech, outside language, the movement of writing may come, under the attraction of the outside" (32), so this attraction to the outside is what pushes Orpheus to his irremediable mistake and, consequently, Eurydice to her eternal limbo.

Still, Orpheus's mistake is moved by his desire and impatience to see and own Eurydice. In Blanchot's opinion, Orpheus can only be himself in his song and this is the reason why "his only destiny is to sing for her":

> He is Orpheus only in the song: he cannot have any relation to Eurydice except within the hymn. He has life and truth only after the poem and because of it, and Eurydice represents nothing other than this magic dependence which outside the song makes him a shade and renders him free, alive and sovereign only in the Orphic space, according to Orphic measure. Yes, this is true: only in the song does Orpheus have power over Eurydice. But in the song too, Eurydice is already lost, and Orpheus himself is the dispersed Orpheus; the song immediately makes him "infinitely dead" [Blanchot, *Space* 173].

In this fragment the Orphic space represents the imaginary space created by Orpheus in his attempt to reach Eurydice again. The distance between Orpheus and Eurydice on their way up to reality is what limits this Orphic space but always in the context of Orpheus's song. In other words, this distance is the space Orpheus's song occupies and, therefore, they both can only exist there. Orpheus's transgression consists in his intense desire to posses Eurydice beyond the limits of his art creation since that space could only be opened by his music.[6] In order to explain this, Blanchot concludes: "He loses Eurydice because he desires her beyond the measured limits of the song, and he loses himself, but this desire, and Eurydice lost, and Orpheus dispersed are necessary to the song; just as the ordeal of eternal inertia is necessary to the work" (172). Remarkably, Blanchot points out two relevant consequences of this aesthetical relation; on the one hand, as creator of the imaginary space, Orpheus gets lost in his piece of art, and, on the other hand, Eurydice, as his piece of creation, is condemned to remain as a ghostly image or appearance since she becomes the result of Orpheus's direct gaze to the heart of night and accordingly, as Blanchot argues: "to look in the night at what night hides, the *other* night, the dissimulation that appears" (172).

As the creator of the imaginary space, Orpheus is condemned to the same loss that Eurydice is and, once both exist only in the imaginary space created by Orpheus, "he is no less dead than she—dead, not of a tranquil wordly death which is rest, silence, and end, but of that other death which is death without end, the ordeal of the end's absence" (172). Eurydice represents for Blanchot his concept of fascination. The separation that exists between Orpheus and Eurydice is where fascination reigns (31). However, it is through the act of seeing how the separation is kept and the attraction established. In this respect, Blanchot affirms: "Seeing presupposes distance, decisiveness which separates, the power to stay out of contact and in contact avoid confusion. Seeing means that this separation has nevertheless become an encounter" (32). Orpheus's gaze establishes an intense contact from a distance and it is through his gaze how he creates an eternal encounter with Eurydice. Although the myth can be interpreted as an irremediable and desperate separation, the French philosopher understands it as an intense encounter in the space of Orpheus's song. Indeed, he explains, "What happens is not an active contact, not the initiative and action which there still is in real touching. Rather, the gaze gets taken in, absorbed by an immobile movement and a depthless deep. What is given us by this contact at a distance is the image, and fascination is passion for the image" (32). Orpheus's look is pushed by his intense desire so Eurydice becomes his fascination and in this "contact at a distance" brings Eurydice back as a result but in the form of an image. In literary terms, Eurydice becomes Orpheus's creation and image, playing the role of that other or *autrui* that inhabits the Orphic space but in the form of someone else.

With Orpheus's gaze, everything goes back to its origin and, in this sense, as Blanchot affirms "writing begins with Orpheus's gaze" and it involves the beginning of the imaginary space. However, Blanchot insists that there is no way in which the writer or creator can reach this precise instant of inspiration unless the writer or creator has the ability to control art or, in the case of the writer, the task of writing. The individual, in his writing operation, can write "only if one reaches that instant which nevertheless one can only approach in the space opened by the movement of writing. To write, one has to write already" (176). This stage, indispensable for the act of writing, can be understood as the step necessary to "approach the space opened by the movement of writing," so it is only when that realm is reached when the inspirational leap occurs.

According to Timothy Clark, in Blanchot's theory of literature, the work desperately looks for its origin in the same way that Orpheus descends to the underworld in search for his lover. This is the reason why Eurydice is the "center of night," that is, the center of the work, and therefore the origin the writer is longing to reach. In Blanchot's words: "The central point of the work is the work as origin, the point which cannot be reached, yet the only one which is worth reaching. This point is the sovereign requirement. One can approach it only by means of the completed work, but one can complete the work only by means of the approach" (54–55). In this way, the gaze of Orpheus would represent the origin and essence of the work. In this context, Clark concludes that "inspiration is both the origin of the work yet also, in its purest and most singular form, its paralysis and ruination, confronting the work with impossibility" (Clark 255) and emphasizes what the myth of Orpheus implies for the definition of inspiration:

> This is the gaze of Orpheus—the moment at which, skillfully leading Eurydice up from the underworld by force of his art, Orpheus, through desire and perverse impulse, cannot not look back at her, even at the cost of ruining his enterprise and losing her. The work may become a "sacrifice" to inspiration, and inspiration itself becomes "the gift par excellence" (*Space of Literature*, p. 175) in Bataille's sense of a giving so extreme that, giving itself, it breaks with any logic of restitution, or any economy of adequation or measure [255].

Through the myth of Orpheus, Blanchot defines the concept of the origin that also Clark remarks being the unavoidable failure of the writer. As he affirms, "the desire and perverse impulse" condemn the work of art to an impossibility necessary to reach the origin of the work that is, essentially, the moment of inspiration. In relation to this, Clark asserts: "To look at Eurydice and to lose her is the exorbitant point and risk to which the work tends, at which it becomes impossible, and hence also the source whence it comes. This is, in short, Blanchot's definition of inspiration"[7] (256).

Ihab Hassan's The Dismemberment of Orpheus *(1982)*

In his work *The Dismemberment of Orpheus* (1982), Ihab Hassan takes the myth of the dismemberment of Orpheus in order to explain a crisis in the art and conscience of modernism and to justify the transition to a postmodernist era. At the end of his work, Hassan proposes the following question: "does the dismemberment of Orpheus prove no more than the mind's need to make but one more construction of life's mutabilities and human mortality?" (271). In order to answer this question, he explains at the beginning of his work that "the crime of Orpheus corresponds to the form of his atonement. Whatever that sin may be, language and form, expressions of an emergent consciousness, are complicit in it" (5). In this way, Hassan connects the moral of the myth with language and, like Blanchot, bases most of his thesis on Orpheus's sacrifice. As it occurs in Blanchot's proposal, Hassan focuses his argument on Orpheus's art and his ability to create a space in which contradictions seem to collapse and unite in only one voice. Again, the contradiction becomes extremely relevant for Hassan as it is for Blanchot, the transgression of the Gods' law which becomes the essential and paradoxical sacrifice to open the orphic space. In this context, Hassan proposes:

> Singing Orpheus restores himself to nature, and moves with the secret life of things. His lyre carries the music of universal harmony and eternal response. Seized by the god, he speaks in no voice of his own; possessed, he loses his self-possession [...]. The mystery unites all opposites, and bursts there where being and nothingness seem to touch. This is why the pure Orphic voice always speaks as one [5].

For Hassan, "vanishing Orpheus leaves behind a lyre without strings; the modern inherit it" (6), which is a statement he translates as a silence that postmodernists have to rescue and reshape. This is the reason why he states that "the forms of silence engage one another, and silence itself suddenly turns into speech" (8). In his definition of silence and speech, Hassan considers what he calls the "negative," an important aspect, a concept he adopts from the nihilistic nature of modern discourse, and concludes that "the language of silence conjoins the need both of autodestruction and self-transcendence" (12). Thus, Hassan proposes the literature of silence as a way of understanding literature from the Marquis de Sade to Samuel Beckett and in it he distinguishes between the artistic movements: the avant-garde, the modern and the postmodern (266). Among the different concepts he develops in order to define a literature of silence, the most significant are, first of all, the fact that for him "ordinary discourse ceases to carry the burden of meaning," and "silence de-realizes the world" (266). Also, it "encourages the metamorphosis of appearance and reality, the perpetual fusion and confusion of identities, till nothing—or so it seems—remains" (13–14). At this point of his study, Hassan introduces Blanchot's work as the example of the practice of the literature of silence, specifically in the context of postmodern literature. In Hassan words, Blanchot's novels and essays work on the "authority of silence" as a way to justify the limits and impossibility of literature, which illustrate the "necessary failure of art" (19) as in the myth of Orpheus. In this respect, he asserts that "Eurydice, for instance, represents the obscure 'point' toward which art, desire, death and night seem to tend; she represents the silence that Orpheus must, and cannot, attain" (19). Likewise, he believes Blanchot is a clear example of the author for whom "negation is inherent in language itself" (19) and whose work "traces the modern will of literature to 'disappearance,' and envisages an "era without words" (19).

Apart from being an example of postmodern literature, Blanchot's work becomes the origin of Hassan's thesis in the sense that whereas Blanchot presents Orpheus's mistake as the inspiration to open the space of literature, Hassan takes this origin and reinterprets the myth of Orpheus, but from the end—that is, the moment in which the Maenads, in an uncontrollable jealous reaction, tear him limb by limb—in order to define the postmodern era of literature. Regarding this, he affirms that "the dismemberment of Orpheus may be a continuous process, and literature may make and unmake itself forever. This view accords with the cyclical nature of the myth" (247). This idea supports Blanchot's thesis about the cyclical nature of the work of fiction. Consequently, Hassan proposes a possible definition for postmodernism as a period that "wishes to surpass or suppress, modernism itself," however, he also assumes that "modernism and postmodernism are not separated by an Iron Curtain or Chinese Wall; for history is a palimpsest, and culture is permeable to time past, time present, and time future" (264).

Eurydice as the Created Object

There is an intimate connection between the concept of image and the figure of Eurydice. In the first sections of *The Space of Literature*, Blanchot relates the idea of image with an uncontrollable fascination or attraction towards the object of creation. Here, Blanchot illustrates the idea of fascination with Orpheus's strong impulse towards his inevitable mistake: to look back at Eurydice. In one of his appendixes titled "The Two Versions of the Imaginary," Maurice Blanchot answers to the question "what is an image?" in the following terms: "when there is nothing, the image finds in this nothing its necessary condition, but there it disappears. The image needs the neutrality and the fading of the world" (Blanchot, *Space* 254). Furthermore, the image, as he states, "speaks to us, and seems to speak intimately to us of ourselves" (Blanchot, *Space* 254), so this moment of extreme intimacy and withdrawal opens a realm which "continues to affirm things in their disappearance" (254). In this context, the only possible existence for Eurydice is when nothing is possible and, therefore, in the neutrality and absence of the fading world. This argument would justify Orpheus's mistake since the only possible way for Eurydice to exist is in the form of an image and in order for that to happen, she needs to do it in the context of a vanishing world.[8]

However, Blanchot affirms that one of the functions of the image is humanizing the formless; to give the nothing a shape in some way recalls the "indelible residue of the being" (255). In relation to this, he adds that "the image cleanses this residue" and makes the individual believe that "separated from the real and immediately behind it, we find, as pure pleasure and superb satisfaction, the transparent eternity of the unreal" (255). Eurydice stands for this kind of "humanized formless nothingness" that remains of her after Orpheus looks at her and this would justify her ghostly appearance. In this context, Blanchot concludes by stating "the image, present behind each thing, and which is like the dissolution of this thing and its subsistence in its dissolution" most of the times represents the object in a "luminous *formal* aura" (255).

According to Blanchot, the image always comes after the object— that is, "we see, then we imagine" (255). On the one hand, the act of seeing lets the creator experience the surrender of the thing into its image. That is to say, "the thing we stare at has foundered, sunk into its image, and the image has returned into that deep fund of impotence to which everything reverts" (255). These last words describe clearly the transformation Eurydice suffers in the instant that Orpheus looks at her. Therefore, Eurydice is the image or object of creation consequent to the instant of inspiration. Not only this, but looking at Eurydice implies gazing at the center of night in the night, the instant in which everything is doomed to disappearance. On the other hand, he explains that when he says "after" "the thing must first take itself off a ways in order to be grasped" (255); Eurydice at a distance depicts the instant of inspiration in which she becomes the ungraspable and vanishing image that opens the imaginary.

Blanchot emphasizes the connection between the essence of the image and death. He insists on a resemblance between the image and the corpse. Indeed he states that "the cadaver's strangeness is perhaps also that of the image" (256). Thus, the concept of death conditions the relation of the image with its space and with others that surround that space. Undoubtedly, Eurydice becomes the perfect character to depict this relation to death and her transformation since, as Blanchot states, "something is there before us"—and in this case in front of Orpheus—"which is not really the living person, nor is it any reality at all. It is neither the same person who was alive, nor is it another person, nor is it anything else" (256). And, in this state of a semi-dead creature, Eurydice loses her notion of space, as she does not belong to the world of the living nor to the underworld since "death suspends the relation to place" and leaves the corpse image in an undefined space: "it is not here, and yet it is not anywhere else. Nowhere? But then nowhere is here. The cadaverous presence establishes a relation between here and nowhere" (256). And, accordingly, the distance between the here and nowhere is the orphic space.

In the section "The Experience of Art" included in *The Space of Literature*, Blanchot makes a brief analysis of Rainer Maria Rilke's work, specifically of his *Sonnets to Orpheus* (1922), and takes one of his verses in order to formulate the most important topics of his theory in relation to the act of writing and the concept of the double. Blanchot quotes the following verse of the sonnets "Be dead evermore in Eurydice" and continues "Be dead ever more in Eurydice so as to be alive in Orpheus," and with it he argues that "art brings duplicity with it." In order to explain this duplicity he asserts that it "invites us to die sadly in Eurydice so as to survive gloriously in Orpheus" (242), a statement that refers back to Blanchot's theory of the "other." In *The Infinite Conversation* he comments again on this topic and explains, "If [...] to write is to pass from 'I' to 'he,' but if 'he,' when substituted for 'I,' does not simply designate another me any more than it would designate aesthetic disinterestedness" (380). Here, Blanchot is presenting a thesis about the narrative voice and the fictional character in the literary text. The "he" is the projection of the artist or, as the French philosopher concludes, the "unlighted event that occurs when one tells a story" (Blanchot, *Space* 381). The narrator, which in this case is the "I" or creator of the story, "is not a historian. His song is the expanse where, in the presence of a remembrance, there comes to speech the event that takes place there" (381). In this context, Blanchot compares the narrator's song with Orpheus's song and asserts that it is in and through it that Orpheus descends to the underworld making of it the speech in which Eurydice becomes Orpheus's projection and creation (381). Blanchot affirms that the nature of duplicity "invites us to die in Eurydice," since in her deadly condition, she represents the transformation into the "he" as a part of Orpheus and that is the reason why she survives in his song and in his figure. In this line of thought, Blanchot adds:

> The "he" marks the intrusion of the character: the novelist is one who forgoes saying "I," but delegates this power to others; the novel is peopled with little "egos"—tormented, ambitious, unhappy, although always satisfied in their unhappiness; the individual is affirmed in his subjective richness, his inner freedom, his psychology [381].

The concept of "he" that Blanchot proposes is a neutral one which "is neither a third person nor the simple cloak of impersonality" (Blanchot, *Conversation* 384). He asserts that "in it, the neutral speaks," and the character itself falls in the present of the narrating speech (385). The neutral, represented by the space occupied by the "he," is defined by Blanchot in the following terms in relation to the narrative space:

> The narrative "he" (il) in which the neutral speaks is not content to take the place usually occupied by the subject, whether this latter is a stated or an implied "I" or the event that occurs in its impersonal signification. The narrative "he" or "it" unseats every subject just as it disappropriates all transitive action and all objective possibility. This takes two forms: (1) the speech of the narrative always lets us feel that what is being recounted is not being recounted by anyone: it speaks in the neutral; (2) in the neutral space of the narrative, the bearers of speech, the subjects of the action—those who once stood in the place of characters—fall into a relation of self-nonidentification[9] [384].

Blanchot concludes that "the narrative 'he,' whether absent or present, whether it affirms itself or hides itself, and whether or not it alters the conventions of writing [...]—thus marks the intrusion of the other—understood as neutral" (385).

Among the main features of the neutral, the French philosopher affirms that "to speak in the neutral is to speak in the distance, preserving this distance without *mediation* and without *community*" (384) because, according to him, "the neutral is precisely the greatest distance governed by dissymmetry and without one or another of its terms being privileged" (386). It is Orpheus's deed and the orphic space that illustrates this phenomenon of a neutral fictional space. At this point the connection between the concept of inspiration and the concept of the other seem to be linked since it is the instant of inspiration that makes the projection of the other possible as a result and product of this artistic moment. This would explain how Eurydice becomes Orpheus's inspiration and double and would justify how, at the end, the duplicity takes place and we "die sadly in Eurydice so as to survive gloriously in Orpheus" (Blanchot, *Space* 242).

Also, Blanchot reflects on Ovid's myth of Narcissus in order to justify his theory about the double. Blanchot focuses on the central event of the story: the moment in which Narcissus sees his image reflected on the water. Whereas it has been assumed, according to what Ovid explains, that Narcissus falls in love with his reflection, Blanchot understands that the consequence of this notorious event for the plot of the myth relies on a different result:

> But the aspect of the myth which Ovid finally forgets is that Narcissus, bending over the spring, does not recognize himself in the fluid image that the water sends back to him. It is thus not himself, not his perhaps nonexistent "I" that he loves or—even in his mystification—desires. And if he does not recognize himself, it is because what he sees is an image, and because the similitude of an image is not Narcissus falls "in love" with the image because the image as such—because every image—is attractive: the image exerts the attraction of the void, and of death in its falsity[10] [Blanchot, *Work* 125].

Again, Blanchot presents the same dichotomy he introduces with the myth of Orpheus but in this case in the figure of Narcissus. Both Narcissus and Eurydice stand for the image result of the instant of fascination that precedes inspiration. Not only this, they also represent that blind spot in which the subject looks directly at the core of essence or the heart of the night and provokes the visibility of the invisible. In relation to this, Michael Newman affirms:

> it is not because he loves himself that Narcissus cannot love another, but rather that, not recognizing his image as his own, he cannot relate to the other, since he has no relation to himself. But this also implies the inverse:

that Narcissus has no self-relation because it is only through the other that
he would have been able to recognize his image as his own [Gill 154].

These lines are supported by Blanchot's thesis: "Narcissus is said to be
solitary, but is not because he is excessively present to himself; it is
rather because he lacks, [...] that reflected presence—identity, the self-
same—the basis upon which a living relation with life, which is other,
can be ventured" (Blanchot, *Work* 127). Thus, he uses the fact that Narcissus does not recognize himself in order to prove that he has no relation with himself and, therefore, there is no chance that he can establish
a connection with the other. Nonetheless, there is another possible
interpretation since he does not recognize himself, as this would have
only been possible through the relation to the other. On these terms,
the myth of Narcissus becomes another example to explain Blanchot's
thesis of the other. Whereas it has been assumed that Narcissus is the
representation of the self-loving and self-admiring behavior, Blanchot
proposes a Narcissus immersed in total ignorance about the existence
of a different self, his most internal part, the one in which death and
alterity coincide.

3

Ghosts
The Writing Inspiration of the Other

One of the most remarkable examples of Maurice Blanchot's theory of inspiration is illustrated in the second volume of the trilogy *Ghosts.* It travels back in time to situate its characters in the New York of 1947, concretely February 3, 1947, the day that Paul Auster was born. As in *City of Glass*, Auster again plays with the mystery novel genre and uses a detective as a central character. Blue, a private detective, is hired by White to investigate the case of a man called Black. Basically, the case consists of watching this man and taking note of his actions. These incidents force Blue to lock himself in a room in front of Black's apartment and watch through his window what he does every single day. Apart from writing, Auster uses ideas such as observation, impersonation and death, which constitute an example of fictionalization of Blanchot's theory of inspiration. Blue will make that apartment into his orphic space, the suitable place for the process of creation where he will reach two important concepts in his task: profound silence and literary death.[1]

Blue's only investigational tool is observation. This is the only way in which he can find clues that become the words that will fill the white pieces of paper of his reports. However, this method turns into a complicated and desperate device when Black's actions are restricted to reading and writing according to what Blue can gauge from his binoculars. The distance that exists between Blue and Black makes everything confusing and unclear. Black's actions are filtered through a glass window that, at some points of the novel, stands for a mirror. Through that window we get an image, an appearance of what Black is doing. It is impossible for Blue to transcribe into words what Black is doing exactly, therefore, he becomes an image of what he is really doing. In order to understand Blue's transcription from a distance, to translate what he sees we can use Blanchot's words in this respect when he explains that "what is given us by this contact at a distance is the image, and fascination is passion for the image" (Blanchot, *Space* 32). Thus, according to Blanchot, the distance is necessary to establish a contact that through the act of seeing will transform into an encounter. Blue is constantly guessing what he sees; he creates images of Black and his actions. Nevertheless, this uncertainty is progressively attracting him to a total distancing from his self and world. Likewise, this withdrawal of the character is due to the fact that Blue is trying to understand the void that rules Black's case. The uncertainty represents an invisibility that Blue is trying to make visible with his interpretations of Black's actions; he is trying to make invisibility visible. The narrator says the following:

> Now and then Black pauses in his work and gazes out the window. At one point, Blue thinks that he is looking directly at him and ducks out of the way. But on closer inspection he realizes that it is merely a blank stare, signifying thought rather than seeing, a look that makes things invisible, that does not let them in [Auster, *Trilogy* 139].

This situation of seclusion takes Blue to Blanchot's essential solitude—that state in which, distanced from the world, the individual is ready to start the process of writing and creation. The process of writing in the novel turns into a metaphor in which the words are projected into the space of the room as an attempt to fill the void with images. Blue is filling the void with images of Black; he is writing the void with fiction. In his attempt to make the invisible visible, his gaze never goes outside towards Black, as Blue believes; it turns back upon itself in a bouncing effect on the window. The look is a door to interiority and circularity where Blue finds out that by trying to make the invisible visible, he is seeing impossibility. This is explained with Blanchot's idea of fascination:

> Fascination is solitude's gaze. It is the gaze of the incessant and interminable. In it blindness is vision still, vision which is no longer the possibility of seeing, but the impossibility of not seeing, the impossibility which becomes visible and perseveres—always and always—in a vision that never comes to an end: a dead gaze, a gaze become the ghost of an eternal vision [Blanchot, *Space* 32].

Blue starts to see in the impossibility of not seeing. If fascination is the solitude's gaze, what Blue starts to be able to see are all those things that are part of his interiority. The look exerts an attraction for Blue through which he is getting closer to death since his process of filling invisibility or recreating invisibility consists of writing.

In the context of Maurice Blanchot's theory of inspiration, both Orpheus and Blue can be compared as two characters that are destined for death, once their creative trip becomes a quest for their artistic inspiration. Moreover, this is possible due to the creativity this vision inspires, meaning images and appearances that become the words that write a new space. It is in this transition passage where Blue becomes "the ghost of an eternal vision." A vision that is himself:

> For in spying out at Black across the street, it is as though Blue were looking into a mirror, and instead of merely watching another, he finds that he is also watching himself. Life has slowed down so drastically for him that Blue is now able to see things that have previously escaped his attention. The trajectory of the light that passes through each day, for example, and the way the sun at certain hours will reflect the snow on the far corner of the ceiling in his room. The beating of his heart, the sound of his breath, the blinking of his eyes—Blue is now aware of these tiny events, and try as he might to ignore them, they persist in his mind like a nonsensical phrase repeated over and over again. He knows it cannot be true, and yet little by little this phrase seems to be taking on a meaning [Auster, *Trilogy* 146].

Blue's look reflects back into his room and gives light to all those things he was not aware of before. In its reversion, the gaze repeats constantly in his mind to remain inside him in an interminable circular effect of beginning and end.[2] The other's look is the individual's look, an inspiration to create the space of fiction. As Blanchot states, it is a direct trip to death:

> To see properly is essentially to die. It is to introduce into sight the turning back again which is ecstasy and which is death. This does not mean that everything sinks into the void. On the contrary, things then offer themselves in the inexhaustible fecundity of their meaning which our vision ordinarily misses—our vision which is only capable of one point of view [Blanchot, *Space* 151].

The Outside, the Night: Writing Blue's Orphic Space

From Blanchot's perspective, the poetic space is "'the road towards myself' that leads to the point where, within myself, I belong to the outside. It leads me where I am no longer myself, where if I speak it is not I who speak, where I cannot speak" (Blanchot, *Space* 156). Parallel to this, Orpheus is the poet, the artist who finds this voice which is his inner self talking, and which he is not able to recognize. That voice is the poetic voice, the voice of literature that is only reachable to the artist in the moment he finds inspiration in his other. The way to create and find that inspiration is by observing. The distance between Orpheus and Eurydice in their way up to the world of the living constitutes the orphic space, and it is comparable to the distance between Blue and Black, the space between those two windows is the orphic space of the novel. Although in most parts of the text Auster suggests that Blue's window is a mirror that reflects Blue himself on the other side, there is evidence in the text which suggests that Black is, in fact, a different person. They meet on different occasions and have the opportunity to engage in conversations. That is the reason why Black can be compared to Eurydice's role in Ovid's myth. Despite this assumption, it is true that Blue identifies with Black in such a way that he can be considered the representation of Blue's real self, which emerges after the process of isolation and writing.

In *Ghosts* the protagonist seems to be the victim of an experiment. Blue is put in a room and forced, by the obligations of the investigation, to write reports of his vigilance. At the beginning, that space is a normal space, which Blue tries to make his own:

> It's a small studio apartment on the third floor of a four-storey brownstone. Blue is happy to see that it's fully equipped, and as he walks around the room inspecting the furnishings, he discovers that everything in the place is new: the bed, the table, the chair, the rug, the linens, the kitchen supplies, everything. There is a complete set of clothes hanging in the closet, and Blue, wondering if the clothes are meant for him, tries them on and sees that they fit. It's not the biggest place I've ever been in, he says to himself, pacing from one end of the room to the other, but it's cosy enough, cosy enough [Auster, *Trilogy* 139].

Everything is prepared for Blue, even the clothes. It seems that White wants to transform him into another person, someone he can control and dress. It is evident that White is the creator of the investigation and therefore the one who decides to control Blue's life. To rule it, he has to disconnect Blue from the world and create a new one for him. This reduced place will be Blue's new existence. As the title reflects, White is transforming Blue into a ghost. Blanchot's concept of a ghost can be associated with the concept of image or appearance that Black also represents. Then, Black, as the narrator states, is for Blue a shadow, someone who, in a way, he invents. In this sense, Black appears in Blue's reports as an image; in his impossibility of seeing what Black is exactly doing, Blue is involuntarily making fiction of Black in his reports.

Blue immerses himself in literature and opens what Blanchot calls the *other night* in his new room, White's ultimate aim. In the same way that Black is Blue's ghost or creation, Blue is White's ghost or creation, because through the excuse of the investigation, White is turning Blue into a writer. In relation to this, Blanchot states, "Apparitions, phantoms, and dreams are an allusion to this empty night [...]. It is empty, it is not; but we dress it up as a king of being; we enclose it, if possible, in a name, a story and a resemblance" (Blanchot, *Space* 163). Nevertheless, that other night has a deep night which represents the outside that will be reached by Blue in his future transgression, when he decides to usurp Black's space and find in it the solution to the case. Blue's transgression is Orpheus's atonement. Blue's usurpation is Orpheus's gaze to Eurydice. This night, in a way, represents the other, opens the door to the other through death. Staying permanently in that night requires, as Blanchot states, one to die, to sleep:

> Every man seeks to die in the world, wishes to die of the world and for its sake. In this perspective, dying means setting forth to meet the freedom which frees me from being, that decisive separation which permits me to escape from being, by pitting action, labor, and struggle against it—thus permits me to move beyond myself toward the world of others. I am, only because I have made nothingness my power: only because I am able not to be. Dying, then, marks the defining limit of this power; it is the grasp of this nothingness and, with this understanding, the affirmation that others come toward me through death [164].

The decisive separation that frees the individual from being is possible through the process of writing. The act of dying becomes only possible when the being, in the other night, melts with his other who represents his real being. With every word he writes, Blue takes one more step towards death.

Ghosts starts with a man named White who walks through the door of Blue's office. Keeping in mind that crossing a door will be Blue's ultimate transgression to Black's room and to the outside, White performs the first transgression of the novel. Passing through Blue's door implies opening a new universe for Blue:

First of all there is Blue. Later there is White, and then there is Black, and before the beginning there is Brown. Brown broke him in, Brown taught him the ropes, and when Brown grew old, Blue took over. That is how it begins. The place is New York, the time is the present, and neither one will ever change. Blue goes to his office every day and sits at his desk, waiting for something to happen. For a long time nothing does, and then a man named White walks through the door, and that is how it begins [Auster, *Trilogy* 137].

Following the scale that the narrator establishes, Blue is the future writer. White represents the piece of paper, which is why Auster chose that name for him. Black is the ink that will fill the white piece of paper and accordingly, Blue's inspiration. Brown is a representation of all those books that "taught Blue the ropes," that educated him in the art of literature. Brown is represented throughout the novel in the figure of all those writers that Auster mentions and which shape the intertextuality of the novel.

Blue's fascination is Black. The character immerses himself in a process of internal exploration in his attempt to understand Black's self. His look at Black's window and image is a constant reverberation which involves an infinite repetition. If to write is to let fascination rule language, Black becomes the ink that will be transformed into those words which become at the end featureless and are drawn upon absence. In this step, those featureless words transform Black and Blue into featureless beings, shadows and ghosts. Blue will melt with words and therefore with Black. Blue and Black's inspirational relationship is explained in Blanchot's words:

To write is to enter into the affirmation of the solitude in which fascination threatens. It is to surrender to the risk of the time's absence, where eternal starting over reigns. It is to pass from the first to the third person, so that what happens to me happens to no one, is anonymous insofar as it concerns me, repeats itself in an infinite dispersal. To write is to let fascination rule language. It is to stay in touch, through language, in language, with the absolute milieu where the thing becomes image again, where the image, instead of alluding to some particular feature, becomes an allusion to the featureless, and instead of a form drawn upon absence, becomes the formless presence of this absence, the opaque, empty opening onto that which is when there is no more world, when there is no world yet [Blanchot, *Space* 33].

The window is a filter of reality. It is also a mirror in which Blue will reflect himself. In the process of writing, the window is a glass that projects another perspective of the same reality—that is, it shows that part of reality which is hidden, invisible. It hides behind it the insight of Blue's report, essential to make the glass transparent and make the visible invisible. When Blue writes his first report the narrator comments about it:

> Words are transparent for him, great windows that stand between him and the world, and until now they have never impeded his view, have never even seemed to be there. Oh, there are moments when the glass gets a trifle smudged and Blue has to polish it in one spot or another, but once he finds the right word, everything clears up [Auster, *Trilogy* 148].

Words and language make things transparent. This means that once they are visible, once Blue can see them, they show a meaning which our vision ordinarily misses. Blanchot calls this moment "the turning back which is ecstasy and which is death" (Blanchot, *Space* 151). This stage is the state reached in Blue's orphic space and that is why the world that he knew stops being represented by the words he uses:

> But then why does he feel so dissatisfied, so troubled by what he has written? He says to himself: what happened is not really what happened. For the first time in his experience of writing reports, he discovers that words do not necessarily work, that it is possible for them to obscure the things they are trying to say. Blue looks around the room and fixes his attention on various objects, one after the other. He sees the lamp and says to himself, lamp. He sees the bed and says to himself, bed. He sees the notebook and says to himself, notebook. It will not do to call the lamp a bed, he thinks, or the bed a lamp. No, these words fit snugly around the things they stand for, and the moment Blue speaks them, he feels a deep satisfaction, as though he has just proved the existence of the world. Then he looks out across the street and sees Black's window. It is dark now, and Black is asleep. That's the problem, Blue says to himself, trying to find a little courage. That and nothing else. He's there, but it's impossible to see him. And even when I do see him it's as though the lights are out [149–150].

This passage can be seen in the light of Blanchot's theory about language. Words obscure the things he is trying to say because words can no longer represent his new world—that is, the space of literature. To protect himself, he starts to enumerate the things he is seeing. Nonetheless, in the act of naming things, he is unaware that he is making them disappear although he thinks he is proving the existence of the world. If we consider them crude words, they represent silence and that is the reason why, when Blue looks out to Black's window, he sees just darkness. In that darkness the other night exists, which is the same night that is invading Blue's room in the form of his own words.

In the context of a linguistic representation and the Blanchotian theory of language, Black represents the meaning, or signified, and Blue the signifier. Black is Blue's signified.[3] Blue is desperately looking for a meaning for his words, and that meaning is Black, who at the same time is the inspiration for his writing. In this case, Blue is the writer that will vanish with his own words, who will stay in that darkness that hides behind his window. Yet, there is evidence in the text that Black is also a signifier, a writer who finds inspiration in Blue's observation. At the end of the novel, in one of his encounters, Black confesses to Blue: "Well, figure it out yourself. My job is to watch someone, no one in particular as far as I can tell, and send in a report about him every week. Just that. Watch this guy and write about it. Not a dammed thing more" (182). Although Black is presented as a different person in his encounters with Blue, Auster is reproducing a fictional projection of him. Accordingly, this means that Blue is a specter as a writer, but Black is Blue's specter. This thesis makes Blue the signifier that will disappear with its signified, Black. There is still one step further in the different layers of the plot. If we assume that the mirror between Black and Blue is put there by White, White would become the signifier of two meanings that disappear in the confrontation between them.

The Double: Eurydice/Black

In Ovid's myth, Orpheus feels desperate due to his wife's death. Love forces him to go to the underworld to bring her back to life. Likewise, his distressing solitude provokes him to make a hopeless prayer to the underworld gods to recuperate Eurydice. He talks directly to death in an attempt to escape from his solitude:

> Here in the end is home; over humankind
> Your kingdom keeps the longest sovereignty.
> She too, when ripening years reach their due term,
> Shall own your rule. The favour that I ask
> Is but to enjoy her love; and, if the Fates
> Will not reprieve her, my resolve is clear
> Not to return: may two deaths give your cheer [Ovid 226].

The extreme desolation that Eurydice's death has caused in Orpheus leaves him immersed in a state in which he can no longer live without his wife. This fact conditions his existence. Due to this terrible event, he finds out that his previous and present existence is no longer possible without another person. In this passage, he suggests that what he is begging for is to be close to her in life or death. Orpheus discovers in full grief and loneliness that a part of him that exists in her has been taken by Eurydice, it exists in her. Auster establishes a relationship between his protagonist and his double, Black, similar to the one Blanchot proposes to explain his myth of Orpheus and Eurydice. Also this implies its eventual consequences of death and disappearance but according to Blanchot's interpretation of the myth in which Orpheus represents the creator and Eurydice the inspiration.

At the beginning, Black exists as a person totally detached from Blue. He is someone who performs different activities independently of Blue's actions. As the novel moves forward, the distance between Blue and Black begins to shorten:

> Black's age to be the same as his, give or take a year or two. That is to say, somewhere in his late twenties or early thirties. He finds Black's face pleasant enough, with nothing to distinguish it from a thousand other faces one sees every day. This is disappointment to Blue, for he is still secretly hoping to discover that Black is a madman. Blue looks through the binoculars and reads the title of the book that Black is reading. *Walden*, by Henry David Thoreau. Blue has never heard of it before and writes it down carefully in his notebook [141].

Some lines later, the narrator tells us that "the only way for Blue to have a sense of what is happening is to be inside Black's mind, to see what he is thinking, and that of course is impossible" (141). This is due to the fact that Blue sees himself as having nothing to do in his case besides watch someone read and write. His unique contact with Black's case is a window that distorts reality. Blue's alternative is to begin speculating about Black's life and to do this he reflects on the etymology of the word "speculate" "from the Latin *speculatus*, meaning mirror or looking glass" (146). Through speculation, Blue will write fiction, will try to fill the void that Black's uncertainty leaves. This draws Blue to a situation in which he starts to write in his notebook about himself, about his experiences and other stories he has learnt during his life. He realizes that the stories "have nothing really to do with Black. This isn't the story of my life, after all, he says. I'm supposed to be writing about him, not myself" (149).

The window is the door that brings Black to Blue's life and the stimulus that moves Blue to the act of writing. The writing process brings Black closer to Blue in an affair that will end in an inseparable connection. On the one hand, as the narrator tells it, Black's life is filled with Blue's experiences and reflections but, on the other hand, it is also filled by new stories Blue remembers. Specifically, two of the stories are parables of Blue and Black as a double but Auster uses the father-son relationship to illustrate it. The first story is about the designer of the Brooklyn Bridge and how he felt very ill before the construction was finished, thus preventing him from walking on his own creation. He leaves the task to his son who also suffers an accident and cannot see the bridge finished. The second story tells the experience of a son who lost his father in the mountains and who finds him frozen a long time after, being the same age as his father was when he died. He is able to see his father's face under the ice as if it were a mirror in which he is reflected. Both stories are metaphors for the relationship established between Black and Blue. The bridge symbolizes the space that exists between them—the orphic space they cross to finally be one person—and the story of the father in the snow is the metaphor that represents the mirror which in Blue and Black's case is the window. To some extent, the stories are reflections of the main plot of the novel, creating a mirror effect.

If the stimulus between Orpheus and Eurydice was their love, the link between Black and Blue is writing through which they will realize they are a part of the same self. In this novel the writers are ghosts and one of those ghosts is H.D Thoreau. The presence of his text, *Walden*, represents solitude—the intention of divesting himself from the world to live in full solitude and where the only activity done is writing. One of Blue's case conditions is solitude inside the apartment. In the loneliness of the apartment, that Someone who inhabits it, is Black. Since the beginning of the case, Blue starts to live Black's life and schedule. The apartment is the space where Blue "has thrown away his life," where he is dead to the people he knew and where he starts the beginning of the end (167). Blue totally forgets his life and his fiancée; he starts a new life without being really aware of what he is doing and that is why he feels so surprised when he meets his fiancée after a long time and she has rebuilt her life. Blue is experiencing Blanchot's "other night" in a walk towards silence and void (the same passage walked by Orpheus with Eurydice behind him). Those steps bounce back on the window and the void is now a presence coming toward Black (Blanchot, *Space* 169). Blue reaches that point in the novel in which he feels totally attached to Black, even stating that he looks inside himself to know what Black is going to do:

In this early period, Blue's state of mind can best be described as one of ambivalence and conflict. There are moments when he feels so completely in harmony with Black, so naturally at one with the other man, that to anticipate what Black is going to do, to know when he will stay in his room and when he will go out he needed merely look into himself. Whole days go by when he doesn't even bother to look through the window or follow Black onto the street. Now and then, he even allows himself to make solo expeditions, knowing full well that during the time he is gone Black will not have budged from his spot. How he knows this remains something of a mystery to him, but the fact is that he is never wrong, and when the feeling comes over him, he is beyond all doubt and hesitation [158].

Blue's reflections are a proof of the bond he has with Black–they are doubles. Not only this, but he also recognizes Black as that part of his self which is essential, because in those moments in which he feels totally removed from Black, he loses the sense of who he is. Thus, his double represents his fictional image, and that is why it is hard for him to recognize himself. Considering Black and Blue to be the same person becomes evident in another passage when the narrator states that Blue finds freedom when he is intertwined with Black:

He discovers the inherent paradox of his situation. For the closer he feels to Black, the less he finds it necessary to think about him. In other words, the more deeply entangled he becomes, the freer he is. What bogs him down is not involvement but separation. For it is only when Black seems to drift away from him that he must go out looking for him, and this takes time and effort, not to speak of struggle. At those moments when he feels closest to Black, however, he can even begin to lead the semblance of an independent life [160].

It is not a paradox, keeping in mind that Black is part of Blue—and a very important part—because he represents the essential part, in the same way that Blanchot explains literature as the manifestation of the essence of language. In the distance, Blue feels crippled inside and trapped by his previous identity.

The text opens another interpretation in which Black is no more than a piece of White's game. With this assumption, Blue concludes two possibilities: either White and Black are working together to conspire against Blue, or White wants to trap Blue, and for this reason, he has placed Black as an insignificant bystander who really occupies Blue's position, with Blue occupying Black's. In any case, there is again a superposition between Blue and Black as interchangeable identities. Yet, there is a further interpretation: White and Black are the same person. This thesis is verified in the text since Blue recognizes common features between them. Also, at the end, he finds all his reports in Black's room assuming that, as White was the only one who had access to them, he either gave them to Black or both are the same person and that is why he has them. At this stage, almost at the end, the novel reaches its most revealing part. Neither disappointed nor deceived, Blue feels that he has found another world through words, the world of nothingness:

> If so, what are they doing to him? Nothing very terrible, finally—at least not in any absolute sense. They have trapped Blue into doing nothing, into being so inactive as to reduce his life to almost no life at all. Yes, says Blue to himself, that's what it feels like: like nothing at all. He feels like a man who has been condemned to sit in a room and go on reading a book for the rest of his life. This is strange enough—to be only half alive at best, seeing the world only through words, living only through the lives of others. But if the book were an interesting one, perhaps it wouldn't be so bad. He could get caught up in the story, so to speak, and little by little begin to forget himself. But this book offers him nothing. There is no story, no plot, no action—nothing but a man sitting alone in a room and writing a book. That's all there is, Blue realizes, and he no longer wants any part of it. But how to get out? How to get out of the room that is the book that will go on being written for as long as he stays in the room? [171–172].

This is a moment of revelation in Blue's new life. He is "half alive," he is already a ghost. This is the real case: to sit a man in a room in solitude, isolate him from his life, and to transform him into a writer who will disappear in the void of his words. The words he has put together on the white sheets of paper in his notebook become fiction, and that is why he lives through the lives of others; he has found a new world in Black. Auster transforms Blue's experience into a metafictional action in the sense that the narrator states, "this book offers him nothing" (the book is the novel *Ghosts*) and he does not want to be part of it anymore. Blue is near to death—the one that emerges from writing. Again, Blanchot's words explain this passage owing to the fact that Blue wants to "leave the chamber," as he wants to write the final chapter with those words that will live forever in silence (Blanchot, *Space* 113). It is Blue's time to transgress Black's space, to turn his gaze to him and die.

The Turn of the Gaze: Orpheus/Blue

Orpheus's crime was to break his deal with Hades, which was to not look back. He was supposed to trust him in his crusade back to life. Apart from causing an infliction, Orpheus's gaze is a transgression to another state or space. According to the myth, he would not be the same person anymore and he would be trapped forever, until the day of this death, in his essential solitude:

> And now they neared the edge of the bright world,
> And, fearing lest she faint, longing to look,
> He turned his eyes–and straight she slipped away.
> He stretched his arms to hold her–to be held–
> And clasped, poor soul, naught but the yielding air.
> And she, dying again, made no complaint
> (For what complaint had she save she was loved?)
> And breathed a faint farewell, and turned again
> Back to the land of spirits whence she came [Ovid 226].

Blue's transgression happens when he decides to break into Black's room, which is the same as invading Black's mind. He is going from his own "night"—the appropriate space to reduce himself to words and create fiction—to the other or essential night to complete the case that ends in Blue's disappearance. Taking action for Blue means to cross the limit and with it "leave the chamber":

> It seems perfectly plausible to him that he is also being watched, observed by another in the same way that he has been observing Black. If that is the case, then he has never been free. From the very start he has been the man in the middle, thwarted in front and hemmed in on the rear. Oddly enough, this thought reminds him of some sentences from *Walden*, and he searches through his notebook for the exact phrasing, fairly certain that he has written them down. We are not where we are, he finds, but in a false position. Through an infirmity of our natures, we suppose a case, and put ourselves into it, and hence are in two cases at the same time, and it is doubly difficult to get out. This makes sense to Blue, and though he is beginning to feel a little frightened, he thinks that perhaps it is not too late for him to do something about it [170–171].

Blue's decision is also provoked by an anxious state of uncertainty. He immerses himself in the writing process but he does not know it, as he is still desperate to solve the case especially now that he suspects that he is the target. However, he is not totally sure of his crime and finds out that action is induced by death: the writing process is getting to an end and Blue is starting to feel that "I can't breathe anymore. This is the end. I'm dying" (173).

As specified by Blanchot, when Orpheus descends towards Eurydice he is to some extent being inspired and, therefore, producing art. Accordingly, art induced by inspiration is opening "the other night." This night stays behind Blue's words but they are only revealed in Blue's transgression of Black's space. Eurydice, under her veil, is the profoundly obscure point toward which art, desire, death and night tend (Blanchot, *Space* 171). Orpheus's work was to bring Eurydice back to life and Blue's was to watch and write about Black. They had to give them shape and reality in life using music and literature respectively. As soon as they fail their job, darkness starts to expand and afterwards occupies everything:

> Orpheus is capable of everything, except of looking this point in the face, except of looking at the center of night in the night. He can descend toward it; he can—and this is still stronger an ability—draw it to him and lead it with him upward, but only by turning away from it. This turning away is the only way it can be approached. This is what concealment means when it reveals itself in the night. But Orpheus, in the movement of his migration, forgets the work he is to achieve, and he forgets it necessarily, for the ultimate demand which his movement makes is not that there be a work, but that someone face this point, grasp its essence, grasp it where it appears, where it is essential and essentially appearance: at the heart of night [171].

Blue decides to impersonate different characters to bring Black closer to him. In his first encounter with Black, Blue is disguised as a homeless man called Jimmy Rose. They have a conversation in which Black talks about the different ghosts or writers that have inspired Auster to write this novel. Black mentions Whitman, Thoreau and Hawthorne, which are ghosts or reflections of the same mirror that multiply in the act of creation. In fact, when Black says to him that he looks like Whitman, Blue answers: "well, you know what they say. Every man has his double somewhere. I don't see why mine can't be a dead man" (174). This is a very significant comment for two reasons. On the one hand, the narrator is referring to all those dead writers who have inspired and educated the real author of the novel, Paul Auster, and who are the ghosts of this novel. On the other hand, as this novel is structured using a mirror effect, these ghosts are also Black and Blue. Black is Blue's double; Blue has discovered this condition through writing and therefore both are reaching death. These encounters are very similar to Quinn and Stillman's father encounters, the only difference being that Quinn did not use a disguise; he just constantly changed his name as a way of disguising himself through different identities.

The second meeting between Black and Blue happens in a club in Manhattan. Blue decides to play the role of a life insurance salesman from Kenosha, Wisconsin called Snow, a very ironic profession keeping in mind that Blue gets closer to his own death every time he takes one step closer to Black. Here is where Blue directly faces the mirror that has followed him through the investigation. Black confesses to him that he is a private detective whose job consists of watching someone and sending in a report about him every week. Black, in his revelation, repeats Blue's thoughts. He tells him that he knows this man more than he knows himself, he just needs to think about him and he knows where he is and what he is doing. In this case, Black is wrong. He thinks his man is at home writing the story of his life when he is actually in front of him:

> So why all the mystery?
> I don't know, says Black, and for the first time his voice betrays some emotion, catching ever so slightly on the words.
> It all boils down to one question, then, doesn't it? says Blue, forgetting all about Snow now and looking Black straight in the eyes. Does he know you're watching him or not?
> Black turns away, unable to look at Blue anymore, and says with a suddenly trembling voice: Of course he knows. That's the whole point, isn't it? He's got to know, or else nothing makes sense.
> Why?
> Because he needs me, says Black, still looking away. He needs my eye looking at him. He needs me to prove he is alive [18].

Blue's look and Black's look are necessary for literature to happen. Their existence is being transformed into what they mean—that is, Blue is getting closer to his signified, dissolving into the signifier he is and represents. He is disappearing into Black's mind and in a way, for literature to be possible, it is necessary to find Black's invisibility and, as his name symbolizes, darkness. In this sense, Blue and Orpheus experience in parallel the inexplicable wish of walking towards death instead of staying in the world of the living. Blanchot explains this in orphic terms:

> But not to turn toward Eurydice would be no less untrue. Not to look would be infidelity to the measureless, imprudent force of his movement, which does not want Eurydice in her daytime truth and her everyday appeal, but wants her in her nocturnal obscurity, in her distance, with her closed body and sealed face—wants to see her not then she is visible, but when she is invisible, and not as the intimacy of a familiar life, but as the foreignness of what excludes all intimacy, and wants, not to make her live, but to have living in her the plenitude of her death [172].

Not to look at Blue or vice versa becomes a disloyal act, but at the same time keeping Blue or Black alive makes the fusion between them and the consequent disappearance impossible. The unique alternative is usurping Black's space:

For it's more than just seeing the room, he knows—it's the thought of being there himself, of standing inside those four walls, of breathing the same air as Black. From now on, he thinks, everything that happens will affect everything else. The door will open, and after that Black will be inside of him forever [186].

Blue's transgression is not to look at Black, but rather to invade his space, considering Black's space as "the other night." Blanchot states that if Orpheus had not looked back at Eurydice, he would not have possessed her. The moment that Orpheus goes down to the underworld, he is not less dead than she is. This death is not the tranquil worldly death but that other death without end, the ordeal of the death's absence (Blanchot, *Space* 172). Besides, Blue, as a consequence of his literature, is living the same death as Orpheus. This is proved in his first meeting with Black when he says to him that he thinks it is possible to have a dead double, indirectly referring to Black as an already dead man. In Blanchot's words, the only possible relationship that Blue and Black can have is through writing:

> Orpheus's error seems then to lie in the desire which moves him to see and to possess Eurydice, he whose destiny is only to sing of her. He is Orpheus only in the song: he cannot have any relation to Eurydice except within the hymn. He has life and truth only after the poem and because of it, and Eurydice represents nothing other than this magic dependence which outside the song makes him a shade and renders him free, alive, and sovereign only in the Orphic space, according to Orphic measure. Yes, this is true: only in the song does Orpheus have power over Eurydice. But in the song too, Eurydice is already lost and Orpheus himself is the dispersed Orpheus; the song immediately makes him "infinitely dead" [173].

When Blue decides to leave the room and confront Black, it is because he thinks that it is the only way to put an end to that book that will be endless unless he gets out of that apartment. According to Blanchot, Orpheus is guilty of impatience. One of his mistakes is his desire to exhaust the infinite, to put a term to the interminable. This is exactly what Blue is doing. The work of art will only be alive if Orpheus restrains himself from looking at Eurydice and if Blue restrains himself from confronting Black in Black's room. However, that is the only transgression that they have to do in order to carry the work beyond what assures it. Orpheus's gaze, and Blue's invasion of space are the only ways in which "the work can surpass itself, be united with its origin and consecrated in impossibility" (Blanchot, *Space* 174). Blue finds this situation when he first steps inside Black's room[4]:

But it goes from bad to worse, and the moment he sets foot in Black's room, he feels everything go dark inside him, as though the night were pressing through his pores, sitting on top of him with a tremendous weight, and at the same time his head seems to be growing, filling with the air as though about to detach itself from his body and float away. He takes one more step into the room and then blacks out, collapsing to the floor like a dead man [190].

At that moment in the novel, Blue discovers that Black's writings are his own reports. He goes back to his room in a state of shock where he returns to his former self. He stops shaving, changing his clothes and looking out the window. Blue has started his agony:

For several days, Blue does no bother to look out the window. He has enclosed himself so thoroughly in his own thoughts that Black no longer seems to be there. The drama is Blue's alone, and if Black is in some sense the cause of it, it's as though he has already played his part, spoken his lines, and made his exit from the stage. For Blue at this point can no longer accept Black's existence, and therefore he denies it. Having penetrated Black's room and stood there alone, having been, so to speak, in the sanctum of Black's solitude, he cannot respond to the darkness of that moment except by replacing it with a solitude of his own. To enter Black, then, was the equivalent of entering himself, and once inside himself, he can no longer conceive of being anywhere else. But this is precisely where Black is, even though Blue does not know it [192].

Blue tidies up his apartment, showers, puts on clean clothes and goes to his final meeting with Black. After a short conversation, Black admits that "you were the whole world to me, and I turned you into my death. You're the one thing that doesn't change, the one thing that turns everything inside out" (196). The climax of the novel arrives when the confrontation between Black and Blue becomes a violent one. Black is threatening Blue with a gun in an attempt of Black to kill Blue and accordingly, commit suicide. Like Orpheus, both are reaching their liberty and the work of literature is happening:

His gaze is thus the extreme moment of liberty, the moment when he frees himself from himself and, still more important, frees the work from his concern, frees the sacred contained in the work, gives the sacred to itself, to the freedom of its essence, to its essence which is freedom. Everything is risked, then, in the decision to look. It is in this decision that the origin is approached by the force of the gaze that unbinds night's essence, lifts concern, interrupts the incessant by discovering it. This is a moment of desire, of insouciance and of authority [Blanchot, *Space* 175].

The moment of authority for Black and Blue is a fight for the possession of the work of literature. It is a battle of roles in which one will be the author and the other one the inspiration. Orpheus makes Eurydice disappear, what he does not know until the end is that he will, in a way, vanish with her too. Blue will kill Black in a fight in which he is killing himself too:

> Blue is too strong for him, all crazy with the passion of his anger, as though turned into someone else, and as the first blows begins to land on Black's face and groin and stomach, the man can do nothing, and not long after that he's out cold on the floor. But that does not prevent Blue from continuing the assault, battering the unconscious Black with his feet, picking him up and banging his head on the floor, pelting his body with one punch after another. Eventually, when Blue's fury begins to abate and he sees what he has done, he cannot say for certain whether Black is alive or dead. He removes the mask from Black's face and puts his ear against his mouth, listening for the sound of Black's breath. There seems to be something but he can't tell if it's coming from Black or himself. If he's alive now, Blue thinks, it won't be for long. And if he's dead, then so be it [197].

This final scene echoes Edgar Allan Poe's short story "William Wilson," which deals with the topic of doubles and fits in perfectly with this one, finishing with the same scene of one double killing the other. As Eurydice wears a veil, Black wears a mask that seems to reveal Blue's face. Blue is unable to distinguish his breath from Black's and knows that whether Black is dead or not, he will not be alive for long. By this time, Orpheus has already seen Eurydice dissolving into the air. While Orpheus's song took him down to Eurydice, Blue's writing takes him to Black's room and back to his own room with all the manuscripts in order to wait for the moment to leave the room. Blanchot, in his interpretation of Orpheus's myth, calls this moment the leap, that is, the moment Orpheus turns his gaze and Blue kills Black:

> Writing begins with Orpheus's gaze. And this gaze is the movement of desire that shatters the song's destiny, that disrupts concern for it, and in this inspired and careless decision reaches the origin, consecrates the song. But in order to descend toward this instant, Orpheus has to possess the power of art already. This is to say: one writes only if one reaches that instant which nevertheless one can only approach in the space opened by the movement of writing. To write, one has to write already. In this contradiction are situated the essence of writing, the snag in the experience, and inspiration's leap [Blanchot, *Space* 176].

What Blanchot calls writing is the moment in which literature completely fills the space of the outside. As he asserts, the only way to get here is through writing: "to write, one has to write already" (176). Words came to Blue across the mirror that the window represented. That bridge governed at the other side by his double Black gave him the inspiration to write a story he knows by heart, because he is the author of it. With Orpheus's gaze and Blue's transgression, Blue's death and disappearance begin. By fusing with Black, by killing Black, he is melting with his signified and therefore he vanishes among the words of his creation. The work of fiction is finished and with it, Blue and the novel *Ghosts* too:

> He reads the story right through, every word of it from beginning to end. By the time he finishes, dawn has come, and the room has begun to brighten. He hears a bird sing, he hears footsteps going down the street, he hears a car driving across the Brooklyn Bridge. Black was right, he says to himself. I knew it all by heart.
>
> But the story is not yet over. There is still the final moment, and that will not come until Blue leaves the room. Such is the way of the world: not one moment more, not one moment less.
>
> When Blue stands up from his chair, puts on his hat, and walks through the door, that will be the end of it [198].

Considering Black the double of Blue, the window stands for a mirror that constantly reflects Blue's thoughts and actions. This generates an infinite movement of repetition which supports the argument that while Blue thinks he is writing about the case and about Black, he is, in actual fact, writing about himself. While Orpheus's transgression is to look back at Eurydice when he is taking her up to the world of the living, Blue's transgression is to conquer Black's space in a confrontation in which Blue kills Black thereby killing himself too. Both write in death once they disappear in Blue's words. Creation is possible in transgression when all the limits are broken and Blue and Black, Orpheus and Eurydice, are free. Nevertheless, this freedom is only possible after the process of writing takes place. Orpheus dissolves with the sound of his music to melt with Eurydice and Blue melts with his words and the inspiration provoked by Black. Ghosts of themselves and shadows of others, Blue feeds his writing from a dead ghost who finally transforms him into one:

> The ghost of Orpheus passed to the Underworld,
> And all the places that he's seen before
> He recognized again and, searching through
> The Elysian fields, he found Eurydice
> And took her in his arms with leaping heart.
> There hand in hand they stroll, the two together;
> Sometimes he goes ahead and gazes back—
> No danger now—at his Eurydice [Ovid 250–251].

4

The Music of Chance
Inspiration for the Construction of a New Universe

The Music of Chance constitutes Auster's fourth novel, a work that, as its title indicates, focuses on the nature of chance, a concept that is present in most of Auster's fiction. Although the text can be interpreted as a discussion of the capitalist system and postmodern society, there are different existential questions that can be inferred in it.[1] In the chapter "*The Music of Chance*: Aleatorical (Dis)harmonies Within 'The City of the World,'" Tim Woods argues, "*The Music of Chance* dramatizes the current feeling of living through a 'legitimation crisis'" and adds that "the text oscillates between the notion that mental and conceptual representations passively reflect the structure of an ultimately fixed and unfaltering reality of essences, and alternatively, the recognition that existence is largely an aesthetic act" (Barone 145–146). This aesthetic aspect of existence is the argument that supports a different analysis of the novel in terms of a postmodernist critique of the capitalist system and introduces a more literary vision of the text in itself.

In most of his novels, the creation of a new literary space comes from the writing and creative activity developed by an author-character. In this case, Auster uses the concept of inspiration to support the construction of a new universe in this novel and again questions the topic of creation. The novel begins with an extract in which Auster suggests that the world the characters are living in is not controlled by them but manipulated by others. The story starts with Nashe, a man who, after receiving a significant amount of money as his inheritance, decides to leave his life behind and travel around America. At this starting point, the text becomes a road novel, or, as Warren Oberman states, "the characters on the open road [...] are condemned to confront the anxiety and dangers that freedom produces, materially and psychologically," and concludes that Auster's intention is to show "the individual confronted within the immensity of his freedom and concomitant responsibility" (192). The setting of the road opens a new universe for this character, first of all because he breaks with his past, and, secondly, because it is the scenario that allows him to meet the character who is going to become his other, Jack Pozzi. In terms of space, Nashe leaves his world behind to inhabit a new one, and it is right at the beginning when Auster specifies all the changes and differences that transgression implies:

> Nashe understood that he was no longer behaving like himself. He could hear the words coming out of his mouth, but even as he spoke them, he felt they were expressing someone else's thoughts, as if he were no more than an actor performing on the stage of some imaginary theatre, repeating lines that had been written for him in advance. He had never felt this way before, and the wonder of it was how little it disturbed him, how easily he slipped into playing his part. The money was the only thing that mattered, and if this foul-mouthed kid could get it for him, then Nashe was willing to risk everything to see that it happened. It was a crazy scheme, perhaps, but the risk was a motivation in itself, a leap of blind faith that would prove he was finally ready for anything that might happen to him [Auster, *Music* 33].

The passage quoted above is an example of inspiration in the text. In the first part, the narrator sates the fact that Nashe's life and destiny are controlled by someone else; in other words, he is behaving like someone else and he is expressing someone else's thoughts. In fact, he states, "as if he were no more than an actor performing on the stage of some imaginary theatre, repeating lines that had been written for him in advance" (33). These lines are evidence that Nashe is no more than a creation of someone else's imagination and—therefore—like other characters in Auster's novels—becomes a fictional character created by another character in the novel. In the last lines of the fragment, the narrator says, "it was a crazy scheme, perhaps, but the risk was a motivation in itself, a leap of blind faith that would prove he was finally ready for anything that might happen to him" (33). Although the narrator is referring to the character's new adventure, he is clearly talking about a leap of blind faith, an action that can be compared to what Blanchot calls the leap of inspiration. In this case, it would explain the entrance into a new world unknown to him since it is the invention of someone who is currently outside his universe but who will control his destiny.

There are three significant moments in the novel—or at least, instants that limit the inspirational experience. The first one is Nashe's decision to leave his life behind; the second would be Nashe's encounter with Pozzi and lastly their arrival to the millionaires' house and their experience with them.[2] During his road trip, Nashe spends almost all his inherited money gambling until he meets Jack Pozzi, who invites him to his last game. Pozzi's intention is to play a poker game with two millionaires and he is absolutely convinced that he is going to win but he needs some money for the bet. Nashe gives him the money he has left and goes to play with him. When he gets into the millionaires' house, there is a clear change of universe:

> As Nashe put his feet on the ground and stood up, an overpowering sense of happiness washed through him. It lasted only an instant, then gave way to a brief, almost imperceptible feeling of dizziness, which vanished the moment he began walking toward Pozzi. After that, his head seemed curiously emptied out, and for the first time in many years, he fell into one of those trances that had sometimes afflicted him as a boy: an abrupt and radical shift of his inner bearings, as if the world around him had suddenly lost its reality. It made him feel like a shadow, like someone who had fallen asleep with his eyes open [59–60].

The narrator is implying the idea of Nashe as a fictional character when he describes him as someone who is feeling "like a shadow, like someone who had fallen asleep with his eyes open," in an atmosphere in which the world that surrounds him "had suddenly lost its reality" (60). At the same time, these feelings are provoked by a transition from one world to another, or in other words, from a world that has been reality for him to a world that has lost it and, therefore, becomes a fictional space. Indeed, the transition is explained as an "overpowering sense of happiness" that "lasted only an instant, then gave way to a brief, almost imperceptible feeling of dizziness, which vanished the moment he began walking toward Pozzi" (59); right after this, "his head seemed curiously emptied out" and he suffers "an abrupt and radical shift of his inner bearings" (59). Here, the character of Pozzi acquires relevance in the context of the construction of a fictional world since he becomes the first element of that irreal atmosphere since it is when Nashe walks towards Pozzi when the "imperceptible feeling of dizziness" vanishes and Nashe is officially inside the imaginary realm. In this context, it is possible to analyze Pozzi as Nashe's "other," as source of inspiration for Nashe's existence in the millionaires' fictional space.

Although this fictional universe seems to be established in the millionaires' mansion, it is evident that Nashe's world changes and was controlled by someone else before. Indeed, the character leaves his previous world behind in order to start a new one in his car on a road trip. He experiences solitude during his trip, a fundamental previous step in order to carry out fiction. The narrator asserts: "he wanted that solitude again, that nightlong rush through the emptiness, that rumbling of the road along his skin," indeed some lines after the narrator states that Nashe, during his trip, "did not utter a single word" (Auster, *Music* 6). Auster is depicting here the isolation of the central character, the solitude required to reach the construction of the fictional world. In this context, the novel shows a progressive development step by step until it achieves the construction of the fictional world: Nashe's detachment from his previous life and isolation from the world. Once this stage is fulfilled, the character is ready to meet his double, Jack Pozzi, who will take him to Stone and Flower, two millionaires that will lock them in their property to construct the fictional world and therefore transform both of them into fictional characters.

It is in their incarceration in the millionaires' mansion when the evidence of inspiration becomes clearer and the fact that Nashe's and Pozzi's world is no more than a projection of Flower's and Stone's imagination:

> He finished the second row of the wall in less than a week, loading up the wagon with three or four stones at once, and every time he made another journey across the meadow, he would inexplicably find himself thinking about Stone's miniature world in the main house, as if the act of touching a real stone had called forth a memory of the man who bore that name. Sooner or later, Nashe thought, there would be a new section to represent where he was now, a scale model of the wall and the meadow and the trailer, and once those things were finished, two tiny figures would be set down in the middle of the field: one for Pozzi and one for himself. The idea of such extravagant smallness began to exert an almost unbearable fascination over Nashe. Sometimes, powerless to stop himself, he even went so far as to imagine that he was already living inside the model. Flower and Stone would look down on him then, and he would suddenly be able to see himself through their eyes— as if he were no larger than a thumb a little gray mouse darting back and forth in his cage [162–163].

This excerpt reveals the idea of inspiration and shows the novel as a creation of a new fictional universe. Here, Nashe is openly talking about a projection of a model Flower and Stone have in actual life; he concludes that he feels as if "he would be living inside the model" and "he would suddenly be able to see himself through their eyes—as if he were no larger than a thumb a little gray mouse darting back and forth in his cage," showing Nashe as a creation of Flower and Stone and therefore, his life and destiny is controlled by them.

Auster constructs the proper atmosphere in order to make the instant of inspiration, and, as a result, the literary space possible. Solitude becomes the first step towards the beginning of a new world, so it is right at the beginning of the novel when Nashe starts his creative passage:

> He wanted that solitude again, that nightlong rush through the emptiness, that rumbling of the road along his skin. He kept it up for the whole two weeks, and each day he pushed himself a little farther, each day he tried to go a little longer than the day before. He covered the entire western part of the country, zigzagging back and forth from Oregon to Texas, charging down the enormous, vacant highways that cut through Arizona, Montana, and Utah, but it wasn't as though he looked at anything or cared where he was, and except for the odd sentence that he was compelled to speak when buying gas or ordering food, he did not utter a single word [6].

The narrator describes a total isolation of the character from his world and from the world in general. From a Blanchotian perspective, this isolation affects language, concretely in this case; the character barely utters a single word except to get the basic needs. In the novel, it is evident that one of the things that makes Nashe feel relieved are the deserted American roads and the sensation of freedom while he is driving, but especially the speed:

> Speed was of the essence, the joy of sitting in the car and hurtling himself forward through space. That became a good beyond all others, a hunger to be fed at any price. Nothing around him lasted for more than a moment, and as one moment followed another, it was as though he alone continued to exist. He was a fixed point in a whirl of changes, a body poised in utter stillness as the world rushed through him and disappeared. The car became a sanctum of invulnerability, a refuge in which nothing could hurt him anymore. As long as he was driving, he carried no burdens, was unencumbered by even the slightest particle of his former life. That is not to say that memories did not rise up in him, but they no longer seemed to bring any of the old anguish. Perhaps the music had something to do with that, the endless tapes of Bach and Mozart and Verdi that he listened to while sitting behind the wheel, as if the sounds were somehow emanating from him and drenching the landscape, turning the visible world into a reflection of his own thoughts. After three or four months, he had only to enter the car to feel that he was coming

loose from his body, that once he put his foot down on the gas and started driving, the music would carry him into a realm of weightlessness [11].

There are two different interpretations for the excerpt quoted above. On the one hand, Tom Theobald presents the idea of speed and the existential effects it has on the central character. In Theobald's words, based on Sartre's notion of freedom, "the speed of driving" becomes a release of the character from all the constraints suffered because of a "unitary notion of self" (92). Warren Oberman offers a similar interpretation of the text in which he affirms that "partly because Nashe refuses to accept the responsibility that his newfound freedom requires, he quickly becomes trapped by his freedom. His experience proves that the inertia of absolute freedom void of responsibility effectively turns into its opposite" (196). Both Theobald and Oberman propose a reading in which the postmodern condition of the character is fundamental and central in order to highlight freedom and its responsibility as two main concepts that define it. Opposite to these two existential proposals, the space of the car becomes central for an aesthetic interpretation: the isolation this reduced space offers him from the world and how he starts to feel a change from his former existence and identity. As in other novels, the room plays a very important part in the process of isolation as a way to start a creative process; in this case, it is the space of the car where the character finds what the narrator calls a "sanctum of invulnerability, a refuge in which nothing could hurt him anymore" (11). Then, the car becomes the ideal place for the protagonist to isolate and start his personal withdrawal process so he can perform his role as fictional character of a different and imaginary world that has been created for him. Here is when the process of identity erasure begins, moved essentially by the required isolation of the character so "as long as he was driving, he carried no burdens, was unencumbered by even the slightest particle of his former life. That is not to say that memories did not rise up in him, but they no longer seemed to bring any of the old anguish" (11).

Bearing in mind that once Nashe starts his trip and shuts himself away in his car the process of fictional creation has started, Nashe already belongs to this new world. Certainly, the narrator asserts: "he had only to enter the car to feel that he was coming loose from his body, that once he put his foot down on the gas and started driving, the music would carry him into a realm of weightlessness" (11). The evidence of the character symbolically losing his body and getting to a "realm of weightlessness" expresses the radical physical and emotional change the character is suffering in order to behave as a fictional character or, in other words, as the creation of someone else. The description the narrator gives of Nashe as someone who starts to become loose from his body and is led to a realm of weightlessness can be compared to the behavior language has according to Blanchot. In the same way language loses its signifier, Nashe is getting rid of his old identity and everything that attached him to the world in order to move to a world ruled by absence, the same that can define the concept of language and literature according to Blanchot.

Nashe's Doubles

In order to illustrate inspiration, it is fundamental to construct the instant that Maurice Blanchot identifies with "the other" or "someone else." In this concrete case, Nashe is already a fictional invention and not the creator of his imaginary space. The same occurs in *Ghosts*, in which the central character Blue becomes the protagonist of a detective fiction created by someone else who, at the same time, confronts him with a double, Black. In *The Music of Chance*, Nashe's double is Pozzi, the man who is going to introduce him to his fictional world. He is the one who will introduce him to Flower and Stone, the creators of Nashe's and Pozzi's future world. The only way in which Pozzi can exist is after Nashe leaves his old self behind. Pozzi would be Nashe's "someone else"; this is the form in which Nashe returns to himself in his solitude. And, this is the reason why Pozzi appears right after Nashe starts his second trip:

> Coming to the top of a slight incline, with a clear view for several hundred yards ahead, he suddenly spotted a figure moving along the side of the road. It was a jarring sight in that bucolic setting; a thing, bedraggled man lurching forward in spasms, buckling and wobbling as if he were about to fall on his face. At first, Nashe took him for a drunk, but then he realized it was too early in the morning for anyone to be in that condition. Although he generally refused to stop for hitchhikers, he could not resist slowing down to have a better look. The noise of the shifting gears alerted the stranger to his presence, and when Nashe saw him turn around, he immediately understood that the man was in trouble. He was much younger than he had appeared from the back, no more than twenty-two or twenty-three, and there was little doubt

that he had been beaten. His clothes were torn, his face was covered with welts and bruises, and from the way he stood there as the car approached, he scarcely seemed to know where he was. Nashe's instincts told him to keep on driving, but he could not bring himself to ignore the young man's distress. Before he was aware of what he was doing, he had already stopped the car, had rolled down the window on the passenger side, and was leaning over to ask the stranger if he needed help. That was how Jack Pozzi stepped into Nashe's life. For better or worse, that was how the whole business started, one fine morning at the end of the summer [19].

This is the moment in which we can consider inspiration to be taking place. Not only because of the encounter between Nashe and Pozzi—that is Nashe and his other—but also because of the feeling of attraction and desire that Nashe experiences: "Nashe's instincts told him to keep on driving, but he could not bring himself to ignore the young man's distress. Before he was aware of what he was doing, he had already stopped the car." This scene is comparable to the episode between Orpheus and Eurydice, not in the tragic way they live it, but there are similar dramatic consequences in Nashe's after he meets Pozzi. As Blanchot states, "To look at Eurydice, without regard for the song, in the impatience and imprudence of desire which forgets the law: *that is inspiration*" (Blanchot, *Space* 173). Contrary to the Greek myth, Nashe does not know that there could be something wrong in his encounter with Pozzi but he suspects it and nevertheless, moved by a kind of uncontrollable force, he takes him in his car. We can compare Orpheus's impatience and desire with Nashe's temptation to stop since both are seduced by the attraction to the other world or, as Blanchot says, "that forbidden movement is precisely what Orpheus must accomplish in order to carry the work beyond what assures it" (174). Thus, in this sense, both accomplish a transgression that is necessary in order to open the other world. So, to do it, it is also fundamental that Pozzi guides Nashe to it.

This being so, Pozzi the *autrui*, is presented as someone who is lost and does not know where he is, that is why the narrator asserts that "he scarcely seemed to know where he was." In the way Pozzi is described, he represents that part of Nashe's identity which is broken and cannot be fixed in the context of a postmodern existence. The fact that Pozzi becomes that "other" that "had been beaten" and whose "clothes were torn, his face was covered with welts and bruises" shows evidence that Pozzi gets into scene in order to reflect that part of

Nashe's identity that he has left behind and did not fit with his old world.

In the same way Pozzi can be considered to be a representation of a part of Nashe's self, he can also stand for that which "is always close to that which cannot be close to 'me': close to death, close to the night" (Blanchot, *Conversation* 215–216). From the beginning, he is described as a strange character whose nature does not seem to be related to the human condition. Auster describes most of the characters that stand for doubles as specters, ghosts or even semi-dead beings that attract his companion to the other side and turn them into these sort of phantoms too. The semi-dead condition responds to a literary stage in the sense that in the moment these characters belong to the fictional creation of another character, their contact with language is direct and therefore, in the context of Blanchot's theory, they represent the absence characteristic of language and accordingly of what constitutes literature. Essentially, this absence is what illustrates the literary death that Blanchot wants to prove in the space of literature. In the text, this is expressed by lines like "Much better, Nashe said. 'You're beginning to resemble something human now'" (23).

After this, Pozzi convinces Nashe to go with him to the poker game he has arranged with the two millionaires, Flower and Stone. When Pozzi explains the situation to Nashe, the protagonist doubts his story and even suggests that he is making everything up:

> "Why should I make it up? The fat one's name is Flower, and the skinny guy is called Stone. The weird thing is that they both have the same first name– William. But Flower goes by Bill, and Stone calls himself Willie. It's not as confusing as it sounds. Once you're with them, you don't have any trouble telling them apart" [28].

The indirect suggestion of Pozzi inventing the whole story introduces in the text the idea of a creation, an alternative new world that both Pozzi and Nashe will be a part of soon. It is true that Pozzi is not the one who creates everything, but he is the one who opens the door to that new world. Apart from this, both Stone and Flower are presented as doubles too, as they share the same name—William. This brief intervention acquires more meaning when the two characters arrive to the millionaires' mansion and Nashe expresses what he feels:

> Nashe understood that he was no longer behaving like himself. He could hear the words coming out of his mouth, but even as he spoke them, he felt they

were expressing someone else's thoughts, as if he were no more than an actor performing on the stage of some imaginary theater, repeating lines that had been written for him in advance. He had never felt this way before, and the wonder of it was how little it disturbed him, how easily he slipped into playing his part. The money was the only thing that mattered, and if this foul-mouthed kid could get it for him, then Nashe was willing to risk everything to see that it happened. It was a crazy scheme, perhaps, but the risk was a motivation in itself, a leap of blind faith that would prove he was finally ready for anything that might happen to him [33].

This passage presents Nashe as a character invented by others. The first lines explain how he feels "he was no longer behaving like himself" or how he feels he is "expressing someone else's thought." Moreover, he states that he feels "as if he were no more than an actor performing on the stage of some imaginary theatre, repeating lines that had been written for him in advance," an affirmation that supports the role of Nashe as a character of someone else's creation. Together with this, Pozzi is explicitly identified as the means through which Nashe enters the other world; in fact, it is the instant that Nashe meets Pozzi, the moment in which he crosses the border to another world:

At that point, Pozzi was simply a means to an end, the hole in the wall that would get him from one side to the other. He was an opportunity in the shape of a human being, a card-playing specter whose one purpose in the world was to help Nashe win back his freedom. Once that job was finished, they would go their separate ways. Nashe was going to use him, but that did not mean he found Pozzi entirely objectionable. In spite of his wise-ass posturing, there was something fascinating about this kid, and it was hard not to grant him a sort of grudging respect [33].

In order to explain the transgression to another side, the narrator uses the expression "the hole in the wall," especially mentioning the image of the wall, something that will become extremely important during their stay in the mansion and the symbol for literary creation. Apart from this, Pozzi is always described in terms of someone who resembles a human image but who is not one completely and the narrator uses words like "specter" to talk about him. The "other" is a phantasmagorical and spectral entity that resembles a human being and that attracts its double or central character to turn into the same nature. This ghostly and incorporeal condition is a symbol to represent language in the text and fictionally illustrates Blanchot's theory. In other words, the "other," and in this case Pozzi, is other-wordly because he is already part of a literary realm and becomes the literary reflection of the central character.

Once the encounter takes place, the narrator shows a progressive union between the two characters always linked to their dual essence; that is, the more they get to know each other, the more things Nashe finds he has in common with Pozzi as if this encounter would be an approach to his own reflection. Nashe explains this mirror effect in the following terms:

> After that conversation, Nashe noticed a shift in his feelings toward Pozzi. A certain softening set in, a gradual if reluctant admission that there was something inherently likable about the kid. That did not mean that Nashe was prepared to trust him, but for all his wariness, he sensed a new and growing impulse to watch out for him, to take on the role of Pozzi's guide and protector. Perhaps it had something to do with his size, the undernourished, almost stunted body—as if his smallness suggested something not yet completed—but it also might have come from the story he had told about his father. All during Pozzi's reminiscences, Nashe had inevitably thought about his own boyhood, and the curious correspondence he found between their two lives had struck a chord in him: the early abandonment, the unexpected gift of money, the abiding anger. Once a man begins to recognize himself in another, he can no longer look on that person as a stranger. Like it or not, a bond is formed [45].

There are two different images expressed in the passage quoted above. On the one hand, Nashe shows a sympathetic feeling towards his new companion, something that makes him trust him more than before and moves him to participate in his new gambling adventure. On the other hand, Nashe admits a clear identification with his partner; he confesses a "curious correspondence [...] between their two lives," and even concludes that "once a man begins to recognize himself in another, he can no longer look on that person as a stranger. Like it or not, a bond is formed." However, these lines also express an exemplification of what Blanchot suggests when he talks about the concept of "someone"—the "he" that is no more than a projection of the "I"—and both become the intrusion of the character into scene. In this sense, Pozzi is the "he" that Nashe as an "I" projects but who is immersed in a creative process in which he comes closer to his other in order to turn into a character. So, the closer they get or the more things Nashe finds of himself reflected in Pozzi, the sooner the transformation into a fictional character takes place. In fact, Nashe talks about him not as a stranger any more and even believes there is a bond established between them that, as he realizes, that he cannot be freed of: "Nashe understood the potential trap of such thinking, but at that point there was little he could do to prevent himself from feeling drawn to this lost and emaciated creature" (45).

Some pages after this episode, the narrator states that "Pozzi had him figured out, and in the end it was almost as though he could read Nashe's mind, as though he were sitting inside his head and watching him think"[3] (51). The double is situated in the mind of one of the characters as a sign that refers directly to imagination and especially to the fact that we are dealing with projections and creations of the mind. Yet again, inspiration is fundamental in the existence of the doubles and it is directly identified with the act of fictional creation.

Nevertheless, it is right before entering Flower's and Stone's mansion when the text seems to explicitly express a radical change in the atmosphere the characters occupy—and, not only that, they also seem to experience a physical and emotional change:

> The air suddenly seemed cooler to him, and a strong breeze was blowing across the ridge, rustling the foliage with the first faint sign of fall. As Nashe put his feet on the ground and stood up, an overpowering sense of happiness washed through him. It lasted only an instant, then gave way to a brief, almost imperceptible feeling of dizziness, which vanished the moment he began walking toward Pozzi. After that, his head seemed curiously emptied out, and for the first time in many years, he fell into one of those trances that had sometimes afflicted him as a boy: an abrupt and radical shift of his inner bearings, as if the world around him had suddenly lost its reality. It made him feel like a shadow, like someone who had fallen asleep with his eyes open [60–61].

Another time, Auster makes reference to a radical change in the atmosphere of the characters and their emotional state in order to explain a transition between two different worlds. Specifically in this excerpt, Auster makes reference again to the fact that the mind of the character is "emptied out" to explain, in some way, the fact that from now on the character's impulses, actions and thoughts are controlled by someone else. The narrator explains Nashe feels that "the world around him had suddenly lost its reality," an affirmation that supports the argument of an opposite existence—if reality is lost, it can be substituted by fiction.

Apart from this, firstly, the narrator asserts that this change in his universe makes Nashe feel like a shadow, what indicates a transformation in the nature of the existence of the character—that is, from what he thought was a real existence to a fictional one in which he is no more than a literary character that shares the same identity features as his double, Jack Pozzi. This shadowy nature is no more than an exteriorization of the linguistic essence of their new existence. Once they are in contact with a fictional realm made of words, they are doomed to a progressive disappearance that starts right at the beginning of their new imaginary life, which is illustrated by this shadowy condition. Secondly, Auster relates this shadowy appearance with the act of sleeping and affirms, "It made him feel like a shadow, like someone who had fallen asleep with his eyes open" (61). The act of sleeping is a fundamental part of what Blanchot defines as *the other night.* "The other night" represents the outside, that place where everything that disappears emerges again in a different shape, which is an imaginary one. Nevertheless, the narrator states that Nashe feels like someone "who had fallen sleep with his eyes open." In order to explain his concept of night and especially *the other night,* which is the one that defines the outside and therefore the literary space, Blanchot talks about the act of sleeping: "here the sleeper does not know he sleeps, and he who dies goes to meet real dying. Here language completes and fulfills itself in the silent profundity which vouches for it as its meaning" (Blanchot, *Space* 163). If we interpret the text using Blanchot's words, Nashe becomes a sleeper and someone who is affected by the nature of language and the silent condition of its meaning. Silent or absent, both concepts explain again Nashe's new shadowy existence always as a consequence of his new relation with language and the trace left by meaning.

Blanchot asserts that "sleep transforms night into possibility," and talks about the concept of vigilance as "sleep when night falls" (265). The concept of vigilance becomes interesting in the sense that it is what, according to Blanchot, seeks for awakening. In other words, an opening, the same that takes place when night leads to *the other night* and opens the new realm. In this way, this is related to the first affirmation in which Blanchot states that "sleep transforms night into possibility," considering possibility as a way to open a new world and cross over it. In relation to this, at the beginning of the novel Nashe considers Pozzi as "an opportunity in the shape of a human being" (33), so another time there is a direct link between Pozzi and the introduction of a new world in the text. In relation to this, Maurice Blanchot mentions the fact that "to sleep with open eyes is an anomaly symbolically indicating something which the general consciousness does not approve of. People who sleep badly always appear more or less guilty. What do they do? They make night present" (Blanchot, *Space* 265). Thus, Nashe's feeling he had fallen asleep with his eyes opened is a sign of his new ability to make night present and hence open a new space.

The first time Nashe and Pozzi see Flower and Stone they "were both dressed in white summer suits. [...] The white suits no doubt contributed to the colonial atmosphere, but once Flower spoke, welcoming them into the room with his rough but not unpleasant American voice, the illusion was shattered"[4] (63). This introduction becomes a signal of their role as the creators of the new world for Nashe and Pozzi, especially bearing in mind that apart from the episode of the poker game, these two characters will stay absolutely separate from the action. Certainly, there are just few occasions in which both Pozzi and Nashe have an encounter with them. In this sense, there is an atmosphere in the novel that leaves open the possibility that the intention of the millionaires was not to play the poker game but to lock them in their mansion and use them to play their game of invention. The first piece of evidence relies on Stone's project. He shows Nashe and Pozzi a model city he has constructed which "in one way, it's an autobiography, but in another way, it's what you might call a utopia—a place where the past and future come together, where good finally triumphs over evil" (72). In it, Stone recreates his own life in a world in which everything is essentially happy and optimistic: "it's an imaginary place, but it's also realistic. Evil still exists but the powers that rule over the city have figured out how to transform that evil back into good. Wisdom reigns here, but the struggle is nevertheless constant, and great vigilance is required of all the citizens—each of whom carries the city within himself" (73).

However, Stone has something more to work in. He is preparing an empty model, a new space that will become the reflection of his own house reproducing each of the places and objects. This is the point at which Nashe and Pozzi play the most important part. Next to this imaginary city stands a blank space destined to be filled with a new model: "As Stone blushed and looked down at the floor, Nashe pointed to a blank area of the platform and asked what his plans for that section were. Stone looked up, stared at the empty space for a moment, and then smiled in contemplation of the work that lay ahead of him" (73). This blank space is thought to become a miniature of the actual house of the millionaires that implies, as Stone himself explains, a reproduction of all the different sections of it. This empty space that has not been filled yet will be constructed with Nashe and Pozzi's experiences in the house. Once the poker game is finished and they are condemned to stay in the house, that blank space will start to be completed. Mainly, he mentions how in this reliable reproduction of the house, there exists a chain of spaces that evidently become an illustration of the mise-en-abyme technique:

> "The house we're standing in now," he said. "The house, and then the grounds, the fields, and the woods. Over to the right"—and here he pointed in the direction of the far corner—"I'm thinking about doing a separate model of this room. I'd have to be in it, of course, which means that I would also have to build another City of the World. A smaller one, a second city to fit inside the room within the room" [73].

As it occurs in other novels, Auster is again presenting the idea of the novel inside a novel which, in this particular example, is mentioned as "the room within the room," an image extremely significant in the context of Blanchot's literary theory. Here, the scenario is structured in different rooms which host different episodes, the city of the world, the poker game and the caravan where the rest of Nashe's and Pozzi's lives will take place. Thus, the "room within the room" is the "novel within the novel"; not only to referring to the millionaires' mansion, the "novel within the novel" starts when Nashe leaves his old life and meets Pozzi, which, therefore, would be the first world to be accomplished and the door to a new one that would open another one.

The poker game with Flower and Stone leaves them broke with a debt of ten thousand dollars. The whole episode of the game becomes the beginning of the work of fiction. It is one of those plots that form the chain of the novel within a novel or, in the case of this text, the room within the room. This novel, apart from those episodes which take place in the road, develops all its scenes in rooms or reduced spaces such as the car, the rooms of the mansion, and the trailer after losing the game. There is a change in the course of the plot once the two protagonists enter the millionaires' mansion. It is as if a transgression of spaces occurs and their existence is altered and controlled by an exterior force. In his study about space in Auster's fiction, Mark Brown states in relation to Stone's and Flower's house:

> The interior of the house, for example, and the resemblances of Flower and Stone to Laurel and Hardy, remind Nashe of a movie set, and reinforce the

107

representation of the house as "an illusion" (Auster, 1992b: 69). This impression is compounded by the mazelike roads leading up to it (Auster, 1992b: 64) and its location in Ockham, Pennsylvania, which, like the town of Cibola in *Mr. Vertigo*, is not on a map. All of these elements combine to emphasize the importance of the cognition of space and the experience of spatiality in Auster's work [133].

In this sense, the text presents different connotations to support the idea that the mansion is in itself already an imaginary place. This would explain why the two characters suffer a transformation of their existence when they enter the space: "an abrupt and radical shift of his inner beings, as if the world around him had suddenly lost its reality. It made him feel like a shadow, like someone who had fallen asleep with his eyes open" (59–60).

However, it is during the game and right after winning it that the two characters, Flower and Stone, take hold of the situation and start to manipulate the lives of the other two characters. There are two fundamental situations held during the poker game. While the game is taking place, the situation is controlled sometimes by the millionaires and other times by Nashe and Pozzi but the crucial thing is that the two outsiders remain most of the time together; in fact, Pozzi considers Nashe to be his lucky charm. Nevertheless, there is a moment in which Nashe decides to abandon the game to rest and goes to have a look at the city of the world:

> Just as he was about to switch off the light and leave the room, Nashe turned around and walked back to the model. Fully conscious of what he was about to do, and yet with no sense of guilt, feeling no compunctions whatsoever, he found the spot where Flower and Stone were standing in front of the candy store (arms flung around each other's shoulders, looking at the lottery ticket with their heads bowed in concentration), lowered his thumb and middle finger to the place where their feet joined the floor, and gave a little tug. The figures were glued fast, and so he tried again, this time with a swift, impulsive jerk. There was a dull snap, and a moment later he was holding the two wooden men in the palm of his hand. Scarcely bothering to look at them, he shoved the souvenir into his pocket. It was the first time that Nashe had stolen anything since he was a small boy. He was not sure why he had done it, but the last thing he was looking for just then was a reason. Even if he could not articulate it to himself, he knew that it had been absolutely necessary. He knew that in the same way he knew his own name [88].

It is not unintentional that he chooses the figures of the two millionaires. If we consider them the creators of the whole situation and especially of the reality Nashe is experiencing in that moment, Nashe's final intention is not only to remove his creators from scene, but it is also to destroy them. In the moment the characters try to destroy their creators, the walls of the fictional world start to tremble and indeed Auster subjects the characters to an imminent death and temporary insanity. In other words, the search of the character for his author implies the end of the novel.[5] Furthermore, in this passage, the narrator explains how "this is the first time that Nashe had stolen anything since he was a small boy. He was not sure why he had done it, but the last thing he was looking for just then was a reason. Even if he could not articulate it to himself, he knew that it had been absolutely necessary. He knew that in the same way he knew his own name," being aware that he had committed a criminal act.

In the context of the construction of an imaginary world, this is an act of transgression, of violation of the limits between the creator and the character created. Nashe is transgressing the limits of his fictional existence and in a symbolic act, takes the two fake figures and puts them in his pocket in a failed act to control them. This argument is probed by Pozzi just some lines after. When Nashe comes back to take up the poker game, Pozzi tells him: "Shit. Don't you know better than to walk out on me like that? You're my lucky charm, asshole. As soon as you left, the goddamn roof started to collapse" (89). On the one hand, Pozzi feels his other has abandoned him. Now that they are in this imaginary world and they are the protagonists, they cannot exist without the other. On the other hand, Nashe himself admits that "as soon as you left, the goddamn roof started to collapse," as a sign of destruction of the space they inhabit now. The possible destruction of this new space comes provoked by Nashe's criminal act as a character. In the instant he takes the fake figures of Flower and Stone, he is trying to destroy his own creators and therefore the only space in which he can be alive in that moment collapses. Apart from this, it is right after this when both lose the poker game and start to be explicitly controlled by Flower and Stone. In order to depict the transition to the literary world, the narrator reflects that transformation in Pozzi's figure: "The birds were waking up outside, and as the first glimmers of light entered the room, Pozzi's bruised and pale face seemed ghastly in its whiteness. He was turning into a corpse before Nashe's eyes" (90). Again, the clue word is "corpse" since it implies that the character is directly connected to a deadly atmosphere appropriate for the literary world he is entering in Blanchotian terms.

Wall Writing

The process of inspiration and creation is completed with the construction of the wall in the second part of the novel. Once both Nashe and Pozzi have lost the poker game and have no way to pay their debts to Stone and Flower, they become the millionaires' prisoners. They decide that the best way Nashe and Pozzi can pay them what they owe them is by building a wall with the stones that once belonged to an Irish fifteenth century castle destroyed by Oliver Cromwell. Nashe's and Pozzi's incarceration and isolation is comparable to the one the writer undergoes in a moment of inspiration, therefore, the construction of the wall stands for the process of writing of which Nashe and Pozzi are the protagonists.[6] The strings of this operation are controlled by Stone and Flower, who are not present in this whole episode of the novel but who decide Nashe's and Pozzi's actions, especially restricting their freedom. Indeed, the reader and the characters can feel their presence since there is no way they can escape, although they tried. On the one hand, the construction of the wall resembles the process of writing. On the other hand, the lack of freedom of the character and his feeling of distress caused by being controlled by someone else out of his known imaginary world questions the independence of the fictional character in the text.

Critics like James Peacock, Steven E. Alford or Eyal Dotan consider chance to be one of the fundamental metaphors of the novel and of Auster's fiction. Firstly, Paul Auster, in his work *The Invention of Solitude*, talks about the experience of casualty as something essential to the everyday life of a person. As a starting point of his narrative corpus, he comments during an interview for Sinda Gregory and Larry McCaffery: "Chance is a part of reality: we are continually shaped by the forces of coincidence, the unexpected occurs with almost numbing regularity in all our lives" (Auster, *Red Notebook* 116). In relation to Auster's reflection about chance, Steven E. Alford asserts, "Lived experience is indeed meaningless; it gains its meaning only through retrospection. The events of lived experience are 'chancy'; what moves them from the realm of chance to becoming part of a causal chain is one's attaching the chance event, through an act of telling oneself one's story, to another, significant event" (Barone 109). This is what Alford presents in relation to a more general consideration of the concept of chance.

110

Apart from this, he connects it with literature and affirms that "chance events in literature are not 'chancy' from the standpoint of the narrator, but are such from the standpoint of the reader, so long as the reader understands the narrative as a story and not a plot" (130). Furthermore, some lines after he concludes, "Chance events in life are events outside the narrative; in literature, there are no chance events, except insofar as they appear that way at the reader" (131).

Chance is treated from a conceptual perspective as a factor that conditions everyday life and affects the course of life events. In this same line of thought, James Peacock reflects on the importance of the idea of chance in *The Music of Chance*, especially since it is part of the title of the novel and affirms that "the novel explores the idea that chance almost seems to attain a sort of logic all its own simply by being so dominant" (Peacock 101). Again, chance is presented as a normal, and in this concrete case, logical, feature that belongs to everyday life experience. Contrary to these opinions, Eyal Dotan defines chance in Paul Auster's novels as a "nearly cosmic force which shapes and directs the lives of the characters and the development of the plot" (Dotan 163), an argument that links chance with the idea of an external domination of the imaginary world, that is, the manipulation of a creator. Some lines after this, Dotan concludes, quoting Baudillard, that chance is something that "comes to life when we find ourselves trapped in a huge game, in a universe full of symbolic chain reactions and empty vertiginous catastrophes," a concept that treats chance as an impulse that only emerges in a symbolic realm (166).

According to this line of thought, chance plays a crucial role in the construction of a literary space. According to Mark Brown, "Chance intervenes in Nashe's adventure early, and marks the transition from one life to another" (103). That is, chance becomes the impulse that takes Nashe from one world to another, an argument that is supported by Blanchot's concept of chance and its role in the construction of an imaginary space. Chance, as a concept and experience, is mentioned in the first page of the novel and in the first paragraph. Nashe's encounter with Pozzi is described as one "of those random, accidental encounters that seem to materialize out of thin air–a twig that breaks off in the wind and suddenly lands at your feet" (1). Some lines after, the narrator tells how "it all came down to a question of sequence, the order of events. If it had not taken the lawyer six months to find him,

111

he never would have been on the road the day he met Jack Pozzi, and therefore none of the things that followed from that meeting ever would have happened" (1). Essentially, chance can imply an uncontrolled series of events that the individual can neither predict nor avoid. The main idea is that chance is ruled by arbitrariness, and, bearing in mind that everything that takes place in the lives of Nashe and Pozzi has been determined by an outside creator, chance in this case can stand for that instant in which everything is changed and manipulated for the sake of the imaginary space.

Here is where Blanchot's concept of chance plays a fundamental part in the analysis of this novel as a representation of his concept of inspiration. According to his study in *The Space of Literature*, "chance is death" and adds that "the dice according to which one dies are cast by chance; they signify only the utterly hazardous movement which reintroduces us within chance" (Blanchot, *Space* 116). Blanchot is reflecting on the instant in which everything turns from what he calls "night" and transforms into a different realm. He states that "chance is the night" and "chance is death," two ideas—night and death—which Blanchot uses in order to define the instant of inspiration. Chance takes place when the "dice are thrown," in other words, the moment when what Blanchot calls "night appears" (Blanchot, *Space* 116).

The concept of "night" refers essentially to language and the void left by the signifier and here is where the metaphor of the wall in the novel plays its most important role. Each part of that castle, each stone stands for that signifier left without any meaning since they do not represent the parts of the castle any more. Once the castle is destroyed, all those parts will be used to construct a new thing—the imaginary world inhabited by Nashe and Pozzi. In this context, chance becomes a parallel concept to inspiration and therefore a metaphor of it; this is the reason why it is so relevant in the title. That is to say, the title implies the music or rhythm of inspiration and accordingly of creation itself. As Mark Brown states, "The title encapsulates the operation of chance in this novel. It also captures the way coincidence and contingency provide the accompanying 'music of chance' to the lives of Auster's characters" (103). Varvolgi's opinion coincides with Brown in the sense that she concludes that Auster's intention with the title is to "accommodate the mess" between music and chance understanding music to be like language and as "a unique, original arrangement of available sounds" whereas chance "is meaningless and unpredictable" (101).

In her interpretation of the wall, Varvogli concludes, "By rebuilding the castle as a wall, Flower and Stone effectively erase its meaning and negate its history," a theory that coincides with Blanchot's idea of language and the appearance of absence in the context of the act of writing. This idea is supported by Brown's opinion about the meaning of the wall in the novel: "stones and walls are consistently associated with words and language in Auster's earlier work" (137). As he explains, Auster uses these metaphors throughout his poetry, particularly in the book of poems *Disappearances* (1988): "the language of stones /... to make a wall" (Auster, *Collected Poems* 137). The meaning of the wall in the novel is intimately connected to the importance of objects in Auster's fiction and how their meaning in the texts is linked to the importance of the wall in the construction of the plot and Blanchot's definition of the object in relation to language. In this particular case, whereas Stone has a "city of the world," Flower is, as he defines himself, an antiquarian: "Willie makes things; I like to collect them" (74). Flower has different rooms in the mansion full of things he likes to collect and has turned the space into a private museum.[7] Here the objects of Flower's collection are "neatly mounted and labeled, each object sat under the glass as through proclaiming its own importance," but Nashe considers this enterprise "a monument to trivia" (75). Indeed, he considers the museum "a graveyard of shadows, a demented shrine to the spirit of nothingness" (76). Moreover, they are "condemned by Flower to go on existing for no reason at all: defunct, devoid of purpose, alone in themselves now for the rest of time" (76). Thus, Flower's objects exist there in his particular museum void of meaning and use.

Again, Auster, with adjectives like "defunct" or "devoid of purpose" is referring to the absent nature of things and, therefore, it is possible to establish a parallelism between these objects, these object's definition and Blanchot's definition of the object always related to language.[8] Yet, objects are fundamental in the novel through Flower's museum. Whereas Stone has a model of a city of the world, a miniature of his own existence, Flower has created in different rooms of the mansion a museum full of objects. According to the narrator, Flower's objects, have no purpose in life anymore:

> Flower's museum was a graveyard of shadows, a demented shrine to the spirit of nothingness. If those objects continued to call out to him, Nashe decided, it was because they were impenetrable, because they refused to divulge anything about themselves. It had nothing to do with history, nothing to do with the men who had once owned them. The fascination was simply for the objects as material things, and the way they had been wrenched out of any possible context, condemned by Flower to go on existing for no reason at all: defunct, devoid of purpose, alone in themselves now for the rest of time [76].

This description of the objects is comparable to each of the stones that once shaped the castle which is currently being restored by Nashe and Pozzi forming a piece of art in the form of a wall. The principal thing that links the objects with the stones is the fact that both denote absence and nothingness. Blanchot in his definition of "crude speech" talks about this silence left by language; individuals, in the silence of language, which is the true essence of it, speak in it in order to establish a contact with the objects that surround them:

> In crude or immediate speech, language as language is silent. But beings speak in it and, as a consequence of the *use* which is its purpose—because, that is, it serves primarily to put us in connection with objects, because it is a tool in a world of tools where what speaks is utility and value—beings speak in it as values. They take on the stable appearance of objects existing one by one and assume the certainty of the immutable [Blanchot, *Space* 40].

Thus, the stones are like signifiers, void of concept but which, in their restoration by Nashe and Pozzi will recuperate meaning as a different thing. In these terms, each stone stands for different words that, in the course of their construction, represent the writing of a new and fictional world being starred in by Nashe and Pozzi.

The construction of the wall is not an easy task. All their work is organized and coordinated by the millionaires through their handyman Calvin Murks. The presence of this character makes the absence of Stone and Flower possible throughout their work on the wall and therefore, the necessary distance of the creators from their work of art, which includes the wall and the world created surrounding it. The process of construction is a hard one, which increasingly turns into a very tough routine in accordance with the high debt and consequently high punishment they have to pay:

> It took them nine days to finish the preliminaries. Then they started in on the wall itself, and the world suddenly changed again. As Nashe and Pozzi discovered, it was one thing to lift a sixty-pound stone, but once that stone had been lifted, it was quite another thing to lift a second sixty-pound stone,

and still another thing to take on a third stone after lifting the second. No matter how strong they felt while lifting the first, much of that strength would be gone by the time they came to the second, and once they had lifted the second, there would be still less of that strength to call upon for the third. So it went. Every time they worked on the wall, Nashe and Pozzi came up against the same bewitching conundrum: all the stones were identical, and yet each stone was heavier than the one before it [117–118].

Explicitly, the narrator talks about an increase in the weight of the stones although they seem to be all the same size. Despite the restoration of the stones of the castle into a wall, it becomes an artistic wall, and at the same time a metaphor for the creation of an imaginary world; there is certain irrationality in condemning the protagonists to do such absurd work, especially if it is done in order to pay a substantial debt. On these terms, there is a certain parallelism between Nashe and Pozzi's destiny with the Greek character Sisyphus. According to Albert Camus in his reinterpretation of the myth, "the Gods had condemned Sisyphus to ceaselessly rolling a rock to the top of a mountain, whence the stone would fall back of its own weight" (119). In Ovid's version of the myth, the character of Sisyphus surprisingly appears in the myth of Orpheus and Eurydice. In it, Ovid explains that Sisyphus stops performing his task in the precise moment that he hears Orpheus playing his song to take Eurydice back to the world of the living. Here, the connection between the two myths in the context of Blanchot's theory is evident. Blanchot discusses how the space opened between Orpheus and Eurydice in the moment Orpheus plays to take her out from the underworld is a metaphor for the instant of inspiration—it is the illustration of the creator and the object created through inspiration. In this sense, Auster's plot in a second reading uses the myth of Sisyphus in order to illustrate a process of inspiration and creation and, connected to it, the myth of Orpheus. This last myth is also present since it is the thesis Blanchot uses to explain and present his definition of inspiration and remarkably Sisyphus intervenes in it in the same way that it does in Auster's plot. Thus, the reinterpretation of the myth of Orpheus and Eurydice can be applied to the two creators, Stone and Flower, who are the ones in charge of controlling and creating this imaginary world in which Nashe and Pozzi are trapped. Music is present throughout the whole experience but in a different way than it is in the Greek myth. Certainly, there is a passage in the novel, after they have lost the poker game, which is very revealing in terms of inspiration and especially in its connection to Orpheus's myth:

And then, just at the moment when things get really bad, it pops into your head to steal a chunk of the model. I can't believe what a mistake that was. No class, Jim, an amateurish stunt. It's like committing a sin to do a thing like that, it's like violating a fundamental law. We had everything was turning into music for us, and then you have to go upstairs and smash all the instruments [126].

In the passage quoted above, Pozzi is again talking about a transgression—in other words, "violating a fundamental law" in terms of the poker game—which can be applied to the literary context. He continues by saying "we had everything in harmony. We'd come to the point where everything was turning into music for us and then you have to go upstairs and smash all the instruments," which is an affirmation comparable to Orpheus's violation of the Gods' law when he turns to look back at Eurydice. In both cases, music is gone and everything turns into appearance. According to Albert Camus in his work *The Myth of Sisyphus* (1942) Sisyphus is the absurd hero (120) and he defines him in the following way:

He is, as much through his passions as through his torture. His scorn of the gods, his hatred of death, and his passion for life won him that unspeakable penalty in which the whole being is exerted toward accomplishing nothing. This is the price that must be paid for the passions of earth [120].

It is interesting how Camus highlights the fact that this is the price Sisyphus pays for "the passions of earth," which is a similar punishment the protagonists are suffering for the pleasure of a game. Some lines after this, Camus asserts that "Sisyphus watches the stone rush down in a few moments toward that lower world whence he will have to push it up again toward the summit. He goes back down to the plain. It is during that return, that pause, that Sisyphus interests me" (120–121). The French writer is interested in this pause since that is the moment in which the absurd hero becomes aware of his situation and therefore knows he is not going to be free of that torture in his life. Camus wonders, "where would his torture be, indeed, if at every step the hope of succeeding upheld him?" (121). Hence, the figure of the absurd hero is aware of the nonsense of his fate. In relation to this, the French writer concludes his study with the following argument:

At the subtle moment when man glances backward over his life, Sisyphus returning toward his rock, in that slight pivoting he contemplates that series of unrelated actions which become his fate, created by him, combined under his memory's eye and soon sealed by his death. Thus, convinced of the wholly human origin of all that is human, a blind man eager to see who knows that the night has no end, he is still on the go. The rock is still rolling [123].

There is a parallelism between the role of the Gods as essential creators and Stone and Flower as imaginary creators. The three of them decide and guide the destiny of some characters, which in this case are Sisyphus, on the one hand, and Nashe and Pozzi, on the other. As Camus explains, "Sisyphus returning toward his rock, in that slight pivoting he contemplates that series of unrelated actions which become his fate, created by him, combined under his memory's eye and soon sealed by his death" (123); this idea is another way of interpreting Nashe's and Pozzi's work since although they have been instructed by the millionaires, they are constructing the wall and therefore generating the area of imaginary space in which they can exist. In this sense, the wall is their space and their fate which can only be surpassed with death. That being so, Nashe and Pozzi's destiny, as it occurs at the end of the novel, is death, and the only destiny that waits for them behind the wall they have constructed is also death. On the one hand, both in the myth and in the fiction, the Gods/creators are the ones who control the characters' lives; on the other hand, as has been mentioned before and as Camus concludes, the only way out from that realm is death, especially if we consider it to be the existence of a literary world. This is how Blanchot interprets Camus's myth of Sisyphus. Based on Camus's work, Blanchot states, "we have called absurd this situation of man who passionately aspires to clarity and unity in a universe where this aspiration is finally always disappointed" (Blanchot, *Faux* 56). This evident feeling of frustration leads the absurd hero to a situation that seems to be ruled by absence:

> From the instant that, with all my strength, I link myself as the only possibility to a universe where my presence has no meaning, I must completely renounce hope; from the instant that, toward and against everything, I maintain my will to see everything clearly, knowing that the obscurity will never diminish, I must completely renounce rest [56].

Blanchot explicitly explains the situation of the absurd hero as one totally void of meaning and hope. Accordingly, it is an existence absorbed by absence and nothingness. In fact, some lines after he affirms, "The absurd man, turned toward nothingness as toward the most obvious absurdity, feels himself foreign enough to his own life to accept it, travel through it, and even enhance it" (57). Blanchot, in his definition of the absurd man and his realm of existence, he is again describing the main features of the imaginary realm. Death becomes the only way out of the condition of the absurd hero in the same way death becomes the only exit from the literary space or, in other words, the final aim of its imaginary condition. In itself, the space where the absurd hero works—that is, Sisyphus's way up the hill to the summit and Nashe and Pozzi's little shelter in the meadow—becomes an imaginary space where impossibility, meaninglessness and nothingness manifest as its main features, that is to say, characteristics that define Blanchot's conception of language and literature. As a result, whereas the myth of Orpheus and Eurydice can be interpreted as a manifestation of the instant of inspiration, the myth of Sisyphus can be interpreted as a way to understand or illustrate the situation of a character trapped in a fiction that is being built by him but neither controlled by him nor created by him.

Throughout the construction of the wall, there are two fundamental episodes which denote the creative and literary connotations of the project. Both of them are related to Pozzi and the relationship established with the other protagonist, Nashe. The work provokes different feelings and reactions in the two of them. Whereas for Nashe it becomes, in some way, a liberating task, something that for the time being gives him stability and an aim in life, for Pozzi it turns into a very hard and nonsensical task he seems almost unable to accomplish to the point that it is Nashe who will do most of the work. Although it is a hard task, as it has been described before, the wall becomes sometimes a little hope in their punishment, something that opposes the frustrated spirit of Sysiphus. However, this hopeful motivation will always be annulled by the absolute impossibility of the two protagonists of ever escaping from the meadow—which, as a result, controls their own lives and fate:

> They put in the thousandth stone on October eighth, polishing off the bottom row with more than a week to spare. In spite of everything, Nashe could not help feeling a sense of accomplishment. They had made a mark somehow, they had done something that would remain after they were gone, and no matter where they happened to be, a part of this wall would always belong to them. Even Pozzi looked happy about it, and when the last stone was finally cemented into place, he stepped back for a moment and said to Nashe, "Well, my man, get a load of what we just did" [134].

The fragment quoted above reflects not only the work the two protagonists are doing with the wall, but also the connection they have with this project. There is a kind of identity connection between them and the stones of the wall. Certainly, the narrator states that "they had made a mark somehow, they had done something that would remain after they were gone, and no matter where they happened to be, a part of this wall would always belong to them" (134). In these terms, they are treated as clear participants in the creation of this piece of art. Not only that, they are key pieces which, without them, there is no way the wall could exist. If we interpret the wall and its construction as the progressive writing of the fiction they are living in, both Nashe and Pozzi belong to the wall in the same way the wall belongs to them— that is to say, there would be no wall without them. Remarkably, Pozzi, in a moment of euphoria, walks on the line of stones as if it were a tightrope situated at a very dangerous height. Pozzi walks on that line of stones in the same way he could walk the sentences those stones form in the corpus of the text that constructs his literary space. In relation to this, Nashe feels "in the verge of tears" as a prediction of what comes next: Pozzi's attempt to escape and the fatal consequences it brings to him. The interpretation of the wall as the metaphor of the writing of a text is reinforced by what Murks adds right after the episode mentioned above:

> "It's really not such bad work," Murks continued. "At least it's all there in front of you. You put down a stone, and something happens. You put down another stone, and something more happens. There's no big mystery to it. You can see the wall going up, and after a while it starts to give you a good feeling. It's not like mowing the grass or chopping wood. That's work, too, but it don't ever amount too much. When you work on a wall like this, you've always got something to show for it" [135].

The movement of the stones described by Murks is a metaphor of the pace of writing: "You put down a stone, and something happens. You put down another stone, and something more happens" as if the laying of stones would be like writing and with every stone that stands for a word, the text in which the protagonists exist would be written (135). The good feeling provoked by the wall is linked to the characters in the sense that the more stones the wall has, the more space they have in their imaginary world to exist and interact. Yet, right before this there is a crucial episode in relation to Pozzi and the creators of the literary space, Stone and Flower. According to the narrator, Pozzi believes the instant in which Nashe stole the two miniatures of Stone and Flower from the model of the City of the World becomes the turning point in their lives since they lose all their good luck during the poker game and the course of their lives changes, which is proven by the subsequent events in the plot. In fact, this event becomes a transgression in literary terms if we interpret the model as a reflection or fictional copy of the world in which Nashe and Pozzi have just entered. After they start the construction of the wall, Pozzi is still obsessed with this event so Nashe decides to burn the figures he stole from the model:

> Without saying another word, Nashe went into the kitchen and retrieved a baking tin, a book of matches, and a newspaper. When he returned to the living room, he put the baking tin on the floor, positioning it just a few inches in front of Pozzi's feet. Then he crouched down and placed the figures of Flower and Stone in the center of the tin. He tore out a sheet of newspaper, tore that sheet into several strips, and wadded each strip into a little ball. Then, very delicately, he put the balls around the wooden statue in the tin. He paused for a moment at that point to look into Pozzi's eyes, and when the kid didn't say anything, he went ahead and lit a match. One by one, he touched the flame to the paper wads, and by the time they were fully ignited, the fire had caught hold of the wooden figures, producing a bright surge of crackling heat as the colors burned and melted away. The wood below was soft and porous, and it could not resist the onslaught. Flower and Stone turned black, shrinking as the fire ate into their bodies, and less than a minute later, the two little men were gone [128].

In the first episode, Nashe only steals them in a symbolic attempt to control the situation, but here the transgression is complete and Nashe destroys his creators. Some lines after, when Pozzi realizes what Nashe has done, he says, "You're out of your mind. I hope you realize that" (129). Although in the text it is explained as if Pozzi were talking about a superstition related to luck and the game, he seems to be the only one who knows the literary consequences this event has for his existence. Once this transgression is complete, their only fate is death, not only because they have symbolically killed their creators, but also because once the wall is finished, the literary text is done, and therefore, the only thing that remains is absence.

One of the fundamental conditions of Auster's construction of fiction inside the novel is the character's attempt to control the space they exist in. Characters, as occurs in this novel, are manipulated by other creators that are characters in the novel, and they are forced, like Nashe and Pozzi, to follow the rules of invention they impose. In this sense, Nashe and Pozzi's incarceration becomes a metaphor of the creator's control over his piece of fiction and the slavery condition the characters suffer in their own space. During the episodes in which Nashe steals and breaks the miniatures of Flower and Stone, the transgression of any of the laws imposed by the creator leads to the end of the fiction and, therefore, the death of the characters. In the case of this novel, the two protagonists experience different ends. On the one hand, Pozzi, in a failed attempt to break his contract with the millionaires, escapes from the meadow and the project with no luck. He is mysteriously returned to the meadow dead. On the other hand, Nashe culminates the project, but once that is finished, the end of the novel suggests a possible suicide of the protagonist. In both cases, the end is death, an unavoidable consequence once fiction is finished according to Blanchot. In other words, Pozzi ends his implication in the fiction once he tries to escape his own imaginary space and Nashe supposedly commits suicide once the wall is finished and there are no more words to go on constructing his existence. In the first place, the narrator describes how the two characters that are doubles separate:

> They ate their last meal together as if they were strangers. They didn't know what to say to each other anymore, and their attempts at conversation were awkward, at times even embarrassing. Pozzi's departure was too near to allow them to think of anything else, and yet neither one of them was willing to talk about it, so for long stretches they sat there locked in silence, each one imagining what would become of him without the other. There was no point in reminiscing about the past, in looking back over the good times they had spent together, for there hadn't been any good times, and the future was too uncertain to be anything but a shadow, a formless, unarticulated presence that neither one of them wished to examine very closely. It was only after they stood up from the table and began clearing their plates that the tension spilled over into words again. Night had come, and suddenly they had reached the moment of last-minute preparations and farewells. They exchanged addresses and telephone numbers, promising to stay in touch with each other, but Nashe knew that it would never happen that this was the last time he would ever see Pozzi [154].

The narrator expresses an evident disconnection between the two characters once one of them is on the verge of abandoning their literary space. Also, the narrator talks about silence and night, two images that predict the imminent arrival of what Blanchot would consider a literary death that, in practical terms, manifests as a total absence or end of the novel. In the case of Pozzi, the literary death takes place in an explicit sense since he dies right after this episode and therefore this is the last time they see each other. Pozzi is out of scene, and only Nashe is left there to finish the task, in other words, to finish the novel.

He is the only worker to finish the wall and in his double work he resembles more the figure of Sisyphus. It is in this last part when Nashe has a revelation in relation to the process of inspiration:

> He finished the second row of the wall in less than a week, loading up the wagon with three or four stones at once, and every time he made another journey across the meadow, he would inexplicably find himself thinking about Stone's miniature world in the main house, as if the act of touching a real stone had called forth a memory of the man who bore that name. Sooner or later, Nashe thought, there would be a new section to represent where he was now, a scale model of the wall and the meadow and the trailer, and once those things were finished, two tiny figures would be set down in the middle of the field: one for Pozzi and one for himself. The idea of such extravagant smallness began to exert an almost unbearable fascination over Nashe. Sometimes, powerless to stop himself, he even went so far as to imagine that he was already living inside the model. Flower and Stone would look down on him then, and he would suddenly be able to see himself through their eyes— as if he were no larger than a thumb, a little gray mouse darting back and forth in his cage [163].

This fragment links writing creation and the figure of the creator. As the narrator explains, "the act of touching a real stone had called forth a memory of the man who bore that name," referring to Stone, one of the millionaires, and therefore connecting the construction and creation of the wall. Furthermore, the narrator even mentions Nashe thinking about the wall, the meadow and himself as a new part of the model. If we consider the model as the reflection of the fiction Stone and Flower are constructing, the narrator is implicitly saying that while Nashe is constructing the wall, the model is also becoming bigger. Explicitly, the narrator states that Nashe feels that he is already living inside the model, and how his creators would look from above at how he moves and interacts every day.

Once the literary task is concluded and the imaginary world is complete, its immediate result is what Blanchot understands to be literary death. In the case of *The Music of Chance*, whereas Pozzi prematurely dies in the hands of someone else or at least that is what can be presupposed by the reader—Nashe takes the option of suicide, an alternative extremely relevant in terms of Camus's myth of Sisyphus and Blanchot's conception of death. If we bear in mind that both Nashe and Pozzi, but especially Nashe, can be considered examples of Camus's definition of the absurd man and a rewriting of his myth of Sisyphus, it is also possible to connect Nashe's destiny with Camus's idea of suicide. According to the French writer, the absurd man feels "an alien, a stranger," and therefore his "exile without remedy" is unavoidable. He defines suicide as the "divorce between man and his life" and compares it to "the actor and his setting," a simile that coincides more with Nashe's case as the character that divorces his imaginary space. Moreover, Camus concludes that "suicide is a solution to the absurd" and, bearing in mind that Nashe's activity can be defined as absurd it is only when it is finished that he is able to voluntarily encounter death (6).

In a way, this is related to Blanchot's definition of death and its relation to suicide. First of all, the French philosopher affirms that the artist "is linked to the work in the same strange way in which the man who takes death for a goal is linked to death" (Blanchot, *Space* 105). In this line of thought, Blanchot explains:

> It seems that both the artist and the suicide succeed in doing something only by deceiving themselves about what they do. The latter takes one death for another, the former takes a book for the work. They devote themselves to this misunderstanding as if blind, but their dim consciousness of it makes of their task a proud bet. For it is as if they were embarking upon a kind of action which could only reach its term at infinity [Blanchot, *Space* 106].

Blanchot compares suicide with art, and therefore Nashe, in his position of character constructing a work of art, is led to suicide as a way to culminate with it. Another fundamental thing that Blanchot mentions is the fact that in both cases—art and suicide—a leap intervenes: "In both cases an invisible but decisive leap intervenes: not in the sense that through death we pass into the unknown and that after death we are delivered to the unfathomable beyond. No, the act of dying itself constitutes this leap, the empty depth of the beyond" (106). At the beginning of the novel, the narrator talks about a leap that, in some way, recalls the last lines of the novel: "And just like that, he went ahead and did it. Without the slightest tremor of fear, Nashe closed his eyes and jumped" (1). Here the narrator seems to imply that Nashe jumps to his new life, however, these lines are connected to the end of the novel: "And then the light was upon him, and Nashe shut his eyes, unable to look at it anymore" (198). This is the instant in which, apparently, Nashe commits suicide and dies, right in the moment his imaginary world finishes–that being so, he dies so his literary existence concludes. Also, Blanchot asserts, "Suicide is oriented toward this reversal as toward its end. The work seeks this reversal as its origin"

(Blanchot, *Space* 106). It is a reversal towards the incessant or the interminable, to go back to the beginning. While the first leap at the beginning of the novel is a leap of inspiration, of entrance into a new life and, accordingly, to a new literary world, the last leap is a jump towards the absence left by words and to some extent, to the same silence that existed at the beginning of the novel.

5

Mr. Vertigo
The Inspiration of the Created Object

Mr. Vertigo, Paul Auster's sixth novel, is a work that, in the context of Auster's texts, distances itself from the others. Rather than dealing with the urban space of the twentieth century and with characters that suffer the consequences of a postmodern existence in an attempt to either survive or write about it, in *Mr. Vertigo*, Paul Auster depicts the America of the first half of the twentieth century with a story that mixes multiculturalism, the Midwest and the reality of American society. It is the story of Walter Clairborne Rawley, an orphan who begs for money in the streets of St. Louis during the late 1920s. The boy meets Master Yehudi, a Hungarian Jewish man who is going to teach the child how to levitate. In order to do that, he is going to isolate Walter in his farm in the city of Cibola. There, the boy is going to meet other characters, such as Aesop, an African American boy, and Mother Sioux, a Native American woman. All of them constitute a family in Cibola that will take care of the boy. On the one hand, as Mark Brown states, "Walt notes the association of Kansas with the mythical Oz, and compares Cibola to it. As a result, the farm has an unreal or dreamlike quality, reinforced by the tricks of weather and geography that hamper Walt's early attempts to escape" (107). This thesis that supports the idea that the farm itself can be considered a fantastic location inside the plot in which the transformation of Walt into the wonder boy will take place. On the other hand, although not all the American identities are represented in the Cibola family, Aesop, Mother Sioux and Master Yehudi represent the different identities that constitute and shape part of the American identity.

Again, as in other novels, Auster raises the theme of identity. In fact, part of the process of levitation consists of erasing one's identity to become someone else, a recurrent topic in Auster's novels.[1] James Peacock defines the novel as a narrative "which is part rags-to-riches tale, part road narrative, and, later on, part revenge tragedy" (141). Truly, Walt passes from misery to richness right after he meets Master Yehudi and teaches him his art; however, the boy will lose his art and come back to vagrancy soon. In this way, Auster represents the fakeness of the American Dream and how that condition marks the construction of an American identity. Thus, Auster presents a criticism of the idea of the American dream or, at least, how ephemeral it can be, especially bearing in mind that Walt starts being a beggar boy and after fame, ends up being a tramp. That being so, Walt's fate was poverty and misery and there is no way he can get out of that. With this, Auster wants to depict the fakeness of the American Dream and how both fame and money are ephemeral. Yet, it is possible to do a different interpretation of the text in terms of how inspiration works and especially how the process of creation takes place.

Contrary to other novels, instead of depicting the process of creation through the figure of the author and his text or even by the construction of a wall—which is what happens in *The Music of Chance*—here Auster presents how one character, Mr. Yehudi, who stands for the figure of the creator, transforms another character into a different person, which is Walter Rawley becoming Walt the Wonder Boy. Auster includes at the beginning of the novel a fantastic location in a realistic setting—Yehudi's farm in Cibola—together with an unrealistic event—Walt's ability to levitate—which is a picture close to magic realism. In this sense, the imaginary atmosphere of the space is already given and therefore the phenomenon of inspiration is focused on the creation of a new person—Walt the Wonder Boy. Furthermore, Auster, this time, illustrates the process of creation in the figure of Walt the Wonder Boy as object created and Master Yehudi as creator.

Here Auster illustrates Maurice Blanchot's concept of creation and inspiration through the character of Walter Clairborne Rawley in four different stages, the first one being his introduction as a beggar boy and how he is transformed into a kind of superhuman creature that can fly. In this stage, Auster uses Blanchot's concept of inspiration in order to symbolize the transformation of the boy from an ordinary individual into Mr. Yehudi's piece of art. This phase is divided into two different stages: Walt as a beggar boy and then Walt as the Wonder Boy. In a third stage, Walt suffers the consequences of losing his creator and therefore he is not only left alone, but he also loses his ability to fly. Here, Auster depicts Walt's downfall through poverty and a new vagrant phase of his life, comparable to the one suffered by Daniel Quinn in *City of Glass* or Marco Stanley Fogg in *Moon Palace*. Finally, in a fourth stage, Walt writes and leaves a manuscript with all of his life experiences as the Wonder Boy and his time in Cibola with Aesop, Mother Sioux and Master Yehudi. In this sense, the first two stages correspond to the isolation, erasure of identity, and hence transformation of the object observed into a piece of art. The third stage symbolizes the interruption of the creative process due to the death of the creator and, therefore, the abandonment of the character in a semi-dead state. To conclude, the last stage presents writing. This time, Auster uses the story of a mysterious Hungarian magician and his project of teaching an orphan how to fly in order to symbolize and fictionalize Blanchot's concept of inspiration and artistic creation.

An Imaginary Transformation

The first two stages that constitute the first part of the novel deal with the figure of Walter Clairborne Rawley and the transformation of his identity. This transformation has one unique aim: teaching him how to fly and making a profit from it. In this context, Auster creates the metaphor of the flying boy in order to depict the concept of Blanchot's inspiration and especially how the object of art does not need to be something explicit, like a novel. Here it is illustrated in the figure of a flying boy, which becomes a fantastic fact. The novel starts introducing the protagonist and creating an unrealistic atmosphere from the beginning so as to make the central project of the plot realistic:

> I was twelve years old the first time I walked on water. The man in the black clothes taught me how to do it, and I'm not going to pretend I learned that trick overnight. Master Yehudi found me when I was nine, an orphan boy begging nickels on the streets of Saint Louis, and he worked with me steadily for three years before he let me show my stuff in public. That was in 1927, the year of Babe Ruth and Charles Lindbergh, the precise year when night began to fall on the world forever. I kept it up until a few days before the October crash, and what I did was greater than anything those two gents

could have dreamed of. I did what no American had done before me, what no one has ever done since [Auster, *Vertigo* 3].

This is the setting in which the narrator introduces Walt's life and it is remarkable how he points out that "the precise year when night began to fall on the world forever" was the same year he learned how to fly.

The first sentences become relevant especially because the narrator mentions the word "night" to explain an obscure and dark period of American history. However, the word night acquires a different meaning in terms of Blanchot's idea of inspiration, in other words, "night" as essence and as representation of the idea of language. The only way in which Walt can be taught to fly is by reaching that state in which, like most of Auster's characters, he must be established in the realm of night and reach the inner part of his identity. This is what Blanchot explains through the concept of essential solitude and total isolation of the individual with the purpose of being able to encounter his most inner self. And, this is what Auster depicts through the total isolation of his characters that, most of the time, experience a deep, decadent and miserable existence so they can meet with their real selves. Here, in *Mr. Vertigo*, the narrator affirms, "Master Yehudi chose me because I was the smallest, the dirtiest, the most abject 'You're no better than an animal,' he said, 'a piece of human nothingness'" (3).

The key part of this excerpt is when Master Yehudi describes him as a "piece of human nothingness"; again, in comparison to Blanchot's theory, it is necessary to work with an individual divested of what surrounds him in order to work on a piece of creation for the purpose of transforming him into a different individual. Actually, in order to make this transformation possible, Master Yehudi forces Walt to go through different tough and complicated tests which—although they are not exactly the same as the ones which were overcome by Hercules—the aim can be compared to the ones imposed on the Greek hero in the sense that both Hercules and Walt have to succeed in a series of stages required in order to become a different person with supernatural abilities. Thus, as the narrator concludes, to be ready to do this, the existential situation of the individual, and of Walt in particular, has to be reduced to the minimum, nearly reach the limit with death and disappearance: "I was scarcely a hair's breadth greater than nothing, a molecule or two above the vanishing point of what constitutes a human being, and since the master reckoned that my soul was no loftier than an animal's, that's where he started me out: in the barn with the animals" (16). Again, as it occurs in other novels, the protagonist is described in terms of an almost disappearing entity, a ghost, or as the text says "a molecule or two above the vanishing point of what constitutes a human being"—descriptions related to the state of absence and therefore death. As Mark Brown affirms, "Walt is driven into himself to look for points of reference there, and forced to examine his most deeply buried inner self. To fly, he must ultimately disconnect his interior self from his body and (literally) let it float free" (107).

At this point when Walt is ready to transform into a different being, but from the inspirational point of view, he is able to become Master Yehudi's object of creation. Right after Walt's failed third attempt to fly, he comments about Master Yehudi:

> Unlike the previous time, I could no longer dismiss his being there as a matter of chance. It was as if he had known I was going to run away before I knew it myself. The bastard was inside my head, sucking out the juices of my brain, and not even my innermost thoughts could be hidden from him [27].

Another time, the character is aware of the fact that someone else is controlling him. In this case, Walt states, "the bastard was inside my head, sucking out the juices of my brain," implying that not only is he controlling all his actions, but he is also "sucking out the juices of my brain" in order to turn him into his piece of creation. In fact, some pages after, Walt asserts, "Master Yehudi had beaten me to the punch again. He'd turned me into a puppet, and the more I struggled to defeat him, the tighter he pulled the strings" (29).

As in other novels, Auster uses the symbol of the puppet in order to illustrate the codependent relationship between the work of art and its creator. Still, there is something remarkably different between them: while most of the other characters are essentially literary creations, Walt is not a literary character but an artistic creation comparable not only to a Frankenstein model but in extension to the relationship between God and his human creations. Hence, there exists a father and son relationship between Walt and Master Yehudi. In the novel, Walt talks about Master Yehudi as a father: "If a man tells you he's your father, even if you know he's not, you let down your guard and get all stupid inside"[2] (41).

This relationship or "paternal bond" as Mark Brown calls it, is manifested again in the moment Walt levitates for the first time. Actually, Brown concludes, "when Walt thinks he has been abandoned by his creator he experiences a fit of panic, rage and grief. His emotional response is so extreme that he enters a state of disconnection able to separate his inner self from his physical one, and he rises from the ground" (109). Even Brown's argument would explain a possible comparison with the creator-creature relationship in the novel *Frankenstein* (1818) since Brown comments on the moment of "panic, rage and grief" that leads the character to a change in his "sense of self" (109) but in the case of Mary Shelley's character, the instant of panic, rage and grief caused by the abandonment of Viktor Frankenstein provokes a killing instinct in the creature that transforms him into a murderer.

In the first phase of his transformation as a creative work, Walt the Wonder Boy fulfills the basic characteristics that the process of creation implies. To start with, he begins immersing himself in the state of vagrancy he is going to repeat right after he loses his creator. This state of vagrancy is marked by the protagonist's isolation that Auster, in this case, immerses himself in the hostile economic and social situation of America in the 1920s. As he has done in other novels, the remarkable withdrawal of the character inside his own world is always conditioned by some concrete social characteristics. In this particular case, it is the Midwest during the 1920s. Thus, Auster offers two different readings of his work; on the one hand, there is a social and political reading of his texts in which he uses isolation and the impossibility of social adaptation for his characters to construct a social criticism of contemporary society; on the other hand, a more theoretical analysis is possible in which solitude and isolation turn into one of the most significant steps of the process of creation—the transformation of Walter Rawley into the Wonder Boy. Auster's metaphor for the literary space or space of creation is this time Mrs. Witherspoon's house, a farm in the middle of Wichita that becomes a fantastic and magical place in which Walt will develop his powers.

Auster's description of the place is relevant for the following reasons: first of all, the protagonist expresses his feelings of entering into another world—specifically, he mentions crossing a threshold and secondly, most of the references about the place and the feelings it awakens in the character are related to death. Together with this, the protagonist describes the place as an illuminated world, characteristics that refer to Blanchot's concept of night and day in relation to inspiration. Here, in the moment the character is moved to this new realm, the real reference of space is lost and Walt seems to walk towards an unknown space: "It was uncanny how fast it happened. One minute, I'd been walking through the streets of downtown Wichita, and the next minute I was lost, stumbling blindly through a white tempest" (30). He is simply caught in a winter blizzard–however, the word "uncanny" and the fact that he is lost helps to construct this mysterious and unknown space that escapes most of the times in reference to reality. He explains his arrival to the house in the following terms:

> After a while, nothing felt real to me anymore. My mind had stopped working, and if my body was still dragging me along, it was only because it didn't know any better. When I saw the faint flow of light in the distance, it scarcely registered with me. I staggered toward it, no more conscious of what I was doing than a moth is when it zeroes in on a candle. At most I took it for a dream, an illusion cast before me by the shadows of death, and even though I kept it in front of me the whole time, I sensed it would be gone before I got there [31].

Again, the description of the place is related to something unreal, out of this world, uncanny and especially connected to death. Moreover, the character is led towards it by a "faint flow of light" and he compares himself with a moth "when it zeroes in on a candle." In the context of Blanchot's theory of inspiration, the use of images such as death and light are essential to support his thesis. To explain the opening of "other" realm that is the space of inspiration, Blanchot uses the concept of "night" concretely as he talks about "the other night." Blanchot explains the existence of the "other night" by the dialectical relationship between night and day and concludes:

> Night is what day wants not just to dissolve, but appropriate: night is thus the essential, which must not be destroyed but conserved, and welcomed not as a limit but for itself. Night must pass into day. Night becoming day makes the light richer and give to clarity's superficial sparkle a deep inner radiance. Then day is the whole of the day and the night, the great promise of the dialect [Blanchot, *Space* 167].

In the same way that the light is what takes him to Mrs. Witherspoon's house, light is "richer and gives to clarity's superficial sparkle a deep inner radiance" because it is when night becomes day.

The process in the novel is the same, Walt travels from his dark and lonely life to the light of the house: "I stepped into the hallway, and everything was so bright in there, so intolerably radiant, that I was forced to shut my eyes" (31). Auster is explicitly illustrating this new world by using the parallelism between night and day proposed by Blanchot. In this context, Walt would be establishing this dialogue between night and day and he would be entering the light of a new realm in which inspiration is possible. Together with this, the protagonist even insinuates for the first time that he might be dead: "I realized that I must be dead myself and had just walked through the pearly gates" (31). In relation to this, Maurice Blanchot asserts: "Only the day can feel passion for the night. It is only in the day that death can be desired, planned, decided upon—reached" (Blanchot, *Space* 168).

The Orphic Space

Analyzing Blanchot's words, it is remarkable that he understands the idea of light as a way to bring to the surface a "deep inner radiance." Blanchot proposes the thesis of the inner essence as he did in his theory of language and literature. The French critic uses the dialogue between night and day to explain the appearance of this essential side that makes art and literature possible. With the purpose of reaching this stage, it is necessary to go through different phases that affect the identity of the individual. Another time, Master Yehudi and Walt Rawley are lonely characters whose behavior is comparable to the pattern of the Blanchotian "essential solitude." The relationship between Master Yehudi and Walt Rawley is that of creator and object created. In this context, once Walt enters the new house as if it where a new realm in reality, Master Yehudi defines clearly the limits of their relationship: "'Now you know,' the master said. 'Wherever you turn, that's where I'm going to be. However far you run, I'll always be waiting for you at the other end. Master Yehudi is everywhere, Walt, and it isn't possible to escape him'" (32). From this perspective, there is no way in which Walt can exist from now on unless under the orders and will of Master Yehudi since Walt is now Yehudi's creation.

Right after his entrance to the house, Walt gets ill and almost dies of a high fever. What seems a normal consequence after his long trip to Wichita becomes a metaphor for the transformation of the character into the flying boy. In terms of Blanchot's theory, the contact with death is essential to let his inner self come out. In fact, Master Yehudi understands the transformation and the training to fly as "the Ache of Being" that "it was bound to strike me down sooner or later. The poisons had to be purged from my system before I could advance to the next plateau of my training" (34–35). Apart from this, in a conversation between Walt and Master Yehudi, the master explains to the boy how suffering is necessary in order to learn the skill of flying:

> "The birds don't suffer. They just spread their wings and take off. If I got the gift like you say, I don't see why it shouldn't be a breeze."
> "Because, my little pumpkin-head, you're not a bird—you're a man. In order to lift you off the ground, we have to crack the heavens in two. We have to turn the whole bloody universe inside out" [40].

In this way, Master Yehudi's intention is to take the inner essence of Walt and transform him into a flying boy. If we take this idea from the perspective of the artistic creation and the instant of inspiration, Master Yehudi is using a metaphor to depict the search for the essence of language to create an artistic object. This idea is based on Blanchot's thesis on the individual losing his own nature and emptying himself so as to let impersonality arise (Blanchot, *Space* 55). From that impersonality the creator works with his object of creation as if it were a blank page.

In his category of object created, Walt has to lose his own nature in order to stop being linked to others or to himself. In the end, he becomes an empty space, a different person and that is the instant in which, according to Blanchot, "impersonal affirmation emerges" and therefore the transformation is completed. Of all the different trials he has to go through to complete the training (most of them extreme tests which combine physical and emotional strength), the most significant one, and the first one he has to overcome, is when Master Yehudi buries him alive:

> So I let him bury me alive—an experience I would not recommend to anyone. Distasteful as the idea sounds, the actual incarceration is far worse, and once you've spent some time in the bowels of netherness as I did that day, the world can never look the same to you again. It becomes inexpressibly more beautiful, and yet that beauty is drenched in a light so transient, so unreal, that it never takes on any substance, and even though you can see it and touch it as you always did, a part of you understands that it is no more than a mirage. Feeling the dirt on top of you is one thing, the pressure and coldness of it, the panic of deathlike immobility, but the true terror doesn't begin until later, until after you've been unburied and can stand up and walk again. From then on, everything that happens to you on the surface is connected to those

hours you spent underground. A little seed of craziness has been planted in your head, and even though you've won the struggle to survive, nearly everything else has been lost. Death lives inside you, eating away at your innocence and your hope, and in the end you're left with nothing but the dirt, the solidity of the dirt, the everlasting power and triumph of the dirt [44].

Walt's experience is initially tormenting and at the end relieving. Blanchot's parallelism with Orpheus's myth works in this situation to explain Walt's contact with death. In this particular case, Walt's orphic space opens in a grave and the scene resembles Orpheus's descent to the underworld.

However, the aim of Orpheus goes beyond bringing Eurydice back to the light of the world of the living, which is explained by Gerard L. Bruns in the following idea: "it is as though Orpheus were responding to a deeper claim, an exigency more powerful than his essentially philosophical task of restoring Eurydice to the light of being. This would be the exigency of writing" (70). In Walt's experience, something parallel to what Blanchot proposes happens in his particular orphic space. Under the dirt, as he describes it, Walt says, "it becomes inexpressibly more beautiful, and yet that beauty is drenched in a light so transient, so unreal, that it never takes on any substance, and even though you can see it and touch it as you always did, a part of you understands that it is no more than a mirage" (44).

It is possible to establish a parallelism between the light and its beauty with the light of being. This light is the opening of the orphic or creative space as it occurs in Orpheus's myth. Another time, the concept of light is brought into the text in contrast with the darkness of the burial, and by extension, dirt and death. In this particular event that Auster depicts through the burial, he is presenting how the object, in his process of being created and re-created, finds a light, the essence that paradoxically is unreal, insubstantial and seems no more than a mirage. Remarkably, the narrator uses words like "insubstantial" or "mirage" that link directly with the final transformation of Eurydice into a ghost or vanishing figure in the instant Orpheus looks at her and hence turns her into his artistic object. Thus, this moment initiates the process of transformation into the flying boy but also opens the creative or orphic space in the novel where Walter Rawley is ready to become Walt the Wonder Boy and fly.

Still, the opening of the orphic space is formed by two different moments in the novel, the first being the instant Walt is buried alive and the culmination of it in his first experience flying. It is in his first levitation when Walt's body becomes ethereal, and this can be considered a metaphor for the transformation of the word into the image. The narrator explains the first levitation in the following terms:

> Mother Sioux and Aesop slept on their beds, oblivious to my rantings and my tears. Somehow or other (I can't remember how I got there), I was down in the kitchen again, lying on my stomach with my face pressed against the floor, rubbing my nose into the filthy wooden planks. There were no more tears to be gotten out of me—only a dry, choked heaving, and aftermath of hiccups and scorched, airless breaths. Presently I grew still, almost tranquil, and bit by bit a sense of calm spread through me, radiating out among my muscles and oozing toward the tips of my fingers and toes. There were no more thoughts in my head, no more feelings in my heart. I was weightless inside my own body, floating on a placid wave of nothingness, utterly detached and indifferent to the world around me. And that's when I did it for the first time—without warning, without the least notion that it was about to happen. Very slowly, I felt my body rise off the floor. The movement was so natural, so exquisite in its gentleness, it wasn't until I opened my eyes that I understood my limbs were touching only air [62].

Significantly, Walt says, "There were no more thoughts in my head, no more feelings in my heart. I was weightless inside my own body, floating on a placid wave of nothingness, utterly detached and indifferent to the world around me" (62). First of all, this excerpt connects with the passage in which the protagonist has his first contact with death when he is buried alive. There is a direct link between his experience with death and the fact that, as a consequence of this contact, his body and soul are governed by an absence that at the same time allows the levitation. So, the whole training is a work with the purpose of emptying the soul and being of the individual. In relation to this, and in the context of the myth of Orpheus and Eurydice, Blanchot concludes: "he is no less dead than she—dead, not of a tranquil worldly death which is rest, silence, and end, but of that other death which is death without end, the ordeal of the end's absence" (Blanchot, *Space* 172). In his explanation of the myth, both Orpheus and Eurydice suffer from a deadly state that is the "the ordeal of the end's absence." Walt has reached this state and it is this deadly absence that provokes in him weightlessness related to nothingness and detachment from the world around him.

At the same time, this new state in the life of Walt also recalls Blanchot's definition of image. In this sense, apart from reaching a state of absolute absence that allows him to fly, the protagonist is also a fictional representation of the concept of image. In other words, Auster uses levitation and the previous stage to reach it in order to fictionalize Blanchot's concept of image and, paradoxically, he chooses a different representation of it since he is not dealing this time with the act of writing. In this sense, Blanchot exemplifies the conversion of the image in terms of Orpheus's gaze and explains how the fatal decision of Orpheus turning back and looking at his lover is the instant in which he liberates "himself from himself," in the same way Walt understands "there were no more thoughts in my head, no more feelings in my heart."

Walt's act of levitation is what Blanchot explains as the freedom released from Orpheus's gaze. Walt, after his experience of being buried alive, has turned now into a mirage and this is the reason why he is free and ready to fly. Together with this, Auster openly talks about Walt's "duplicity" and how he realizes that there is an "other" that is born from his own existence, that is, the person he has become after the first levitation. He is aware that he is not the same person any more and at the beginning feels uncomfortable. Truly, the protagonist talks explicitly about the "other," someone else resulting from his transformation and therefore from the process of creation and inspiration. As in other novels, Walt also has his double. In this aspect, there are two different interpretations. First of all, Walt and Master Yehudi are doubles. Some critics, such as Varvogli or Peacock, believe in a father-son relationship, and the text supports this argument, bearing in mind that Walt is a vagrant and an orphan with no parents. Furthermore, Walt openly talks about him as his father, saying, "If a man tells you he's your father, even if you know he's not, you let down your guard and get all stupid inside" (41). Actually, in the second part of the novel, Master Yehudi will be assassinated, which takes him totally out of action and leaves his character alone in the space of fiction. As he cannot perform his art without him, Walt ends up turning into a writer who tells his own story. Secondly, otherness and duplicity are reflected in the immediate result of Walt and the levitating boy. He explains how he feels right after his first experience flying:

> That was the struggle: not just to master the skill, but to absorb its gruesome and shattering implications, to plunge into the maw of the beast. It had marked me with a special destiny, and I would be set apart from others for

the rest of my life. Imagine waking up one morning to discover that you have a new face, and then imagine the hours you would have to spend in front of the mirror before you got used to it, before you could begin to feel comfortable with yourself again. Day after day, I would lock myself in my room, stretch out on the floor, and wish my body into the air [66].

In the excerpt above, Walt talks openly about the fact that he is a different person. Some lines after this, he comments, "A couple of times, I felt certain that the master saw straight through me, that he understood my duplicity and was lenient only because he wanted me out of his hair" (67). The idea of the other and duplicity is linked to Blanchot's concept of image. Walt has left his former self behind and now is an image in the same terms that Blanchot explains it. Certainly, one of Blanchot's theories explains how one of the functions of the image is to humanize the formless or give absence a shape so it becomes the "inedible residue of the being" (Blanchot, *Space* 255). Moreover, he concludes that the individual ends up separated from the real but immediately behind it (255) or as Walt expresses it, "I would be set apart from others for the rest of my life" (Auster, *Music* 66). So, like Eurydice, right after the fatal look, Walt is now a "humanized formless nothingness" in his role as other. Thus Walt's duplicity will be mainly focused on his nature as an image.

From this point onwards in the novel, Walt the Wonder Boy starts to perform his show all over America. Eventually he improves his technique and becomes more immersed in his work. In the following events after his first experience flying, Walt is already a created object whose only aim is to perform his new skills. In the novel, he expresses it as an existential crisis that distances him from the world:

I threw myself into my work as never before, exulting in the freedom and protection it gave me. Something had shifted inside my soul, and I understood that this was who I was now: not Walter Rawley, the kid who turned into Walt the Wonder Boy for one hour a day, but Walt the Wonder Boy through and through, a person who did not exist except when he was in the air. The ground was an illusion, a no-man's-land mined with traps and shadows, and everything that happened down there was false. Only the air was real now, and for twenty-three hours a day I lived as a stranger to myself, cut off from my old pleasures and habits, a cowering bundle of desperation and fright [143].

In the excerpt quoted above, Walt identifies what is considered in the fictional context of the real world, to be a false place for him where he feels like a stranger. In his condition of object created or fictional character, the only space where he feels comfortable from now on is in the air, which is a metaphorical representation of the space of creation. So, in Auster's illustration, there is a division of the space between the ground that stands for reality and the air that would stand for the imaginary space.

In the second part of the novel, Walt comes back down to reality again in a terrible experience of poverty and isolation. Accordingly, Auster also establishes a dichotomy between ground and air in moral terms. The space of the air makes the protagonist a different person with a wonderful skill that makes him different and special. Parallel to this, the realm of the ground is still attached to the real world and the adversities of reality. There, he is again the vagrant poor boy of the beginning of the novel that did not receive Master Yehudi's training. The whole novel moves between these two different spaces and how they affect the protagonist's nature.

The course of the novel changes when both Master Yehudi and Walt are assaulted, resulting in Master Yehudi's death. At this point of the novel, there is a radical change of space from air to ground, from the imaginary to the reality of the fiction. Master Yehudi's shoulder is injured in the incident, however, and he has been sick with stomach cancer for a long time. His life expectancy is six months and he decides it is time to die. Literally, he says to Walt, "Death isn't so terrible, Walt. When a man comes to the end of the line, it's the only thing he really wants" (220). Nevertheless, the whole problem of Master Yehudi's death is that he asks his own creation Walt to kill him. Here, the situation between creator and object created is inverted compared to other novels.[3] In the case of *Mr. Vertigo*, the creator asks his creation to kill him. Walt does not feel ready to do so and finally it is Master Yehudi who kills himself:

> But he wasn't listening anymore. Still looking into my eyes, he raised the pistol against his head and cocked the hammer. It was as if he was daring me to stop him, daring me to reach out and grab the gun, but I couldn't move. I just sat there and watched, and I didn't do a thing.
> His hand was shaking and sweat was pouring off his forehead, but his eyes were still steady and clear. "Remember the good times," he said. "Remember the things I taught you." Then, swallowing once, he shut his eyes and squeezed the trigger [221].

Contrary to Auster's other novels, the creator in this case decides to kill himself and, therefore, abandons his own creation and his own imaginary space. Blanchot includes suicide as one of the different possible stages in the process of creation. One of the first things that the French critic mentions in relation to art and suicide is the following affirmation: "Not that the artist makes death his work of art, but it can be said that he is linked to the work in the same strange way in which the man who takes death for a goal is linked to death" (Blanchot, *Space* 105). These lines evoke the confession Yehudi makes to Walt when he asks him to kill him: "When a man comes to the end of the line it's the only thing he really wants" (220). In terms of creative work, although it is explicit in the text that Yehudi knows he is going to die due to stomach cancer, this line can be interpreted as the final realization of Yehudi as an artist—his piece of art, Walt, is successfully completed and, therefore, he can leave his work behind. In the comparison between art and suicide Blanchot explains:

> In both cases an invisible but decisive leap intervenes: not in the sense that through death we pass into the unknown and that after death we are delivered to the unfathomable beyond. No, the act of dying itself constitutes this leap, the empty depth of the beyond. It is the fact of dying that includes a radical reversal, through which the death that was the extreme form of my power not only becomes what loosens my hold upon myself by casting me out of my power to begin and even to finish, but also becomes that which is without any relation to me, without power over me—that which is stripped of all possibility—the unreality of the indefinite. I cannot represent this reversal to myself, I cannot even conceive of it as definitive. It is not the irreversible step beyond which there would be no return, for it is that which is not accomplished, the interminable and the incessant [106].

In this excerpt, Blanchot talks about suicide as a radical reversal but at the same time, as something that to a certain extent denies this reversal. On the contrary, the work of art constantly looks for this reversal as its origin. This implies that death loosens one of his or her identity and creates a situation of non-relation to oneself that leaves the individual in a total unreality of the indefinite. In this light, Varvogli states, "The theme of levitation may be read as an inversion of the earlier fall motif, and it is this inversion that produces a comic effect" (159). The fundamental proposal introduced by Varvogli is the interpretation of levitation as "an inversion of the earlier fall motif." In fictional terms, right after Yehudi's death, the protagonist suffers a fall. So, the inversion that Varvogli refers to can be compared to the radical reversal Blanchot talks about in order to explain the difference between the work, that "seeks this reversal as its origin," and suicide that, as a

139

voluntary death "is the refusal to see the other death, the death one cannot grasp, which one never reaches. It is a kind of sovereign negligence, an alliance made with visible death in order to exclude the invisible one" (Blanchot, *Space* 106–107). If we apply this argument to the text, the one who escapes the "other death" is the creator Yehudi and this particular act condemns his creation, Walt, to live in a constant limbo of poverty, suffering, prostitution and different chaotic events that always make him flirt with death but never allows him to reach it. He turns into a different ghost—not the specter he was in the air performing his art, but one that makes the character live in a constant negligence: "the one who is thus struck is no longer I, but another, so that when I kill myself, perhaps it is 'I' who does the killing, but it is not done to me. Nor is it my death–the one I dealt–that I have now to die, but rather the death which I refused, which I neglected, and which is this very negligence–perpetual flight and inertia" (Blanchot, *Space* 107).

In his study *Maurice Blanchot and the Literature of Transgression* (1994), John Gregg focuses on the task of writing as an example for the act of creation. Following this thesis, he finally concludes:

> In the cases of both suicide and writing, what begins as a concerted act of the will is transformed into fascination, indecision, and passivity. The English phrase "suicide victim" aptly describes this transformation from active to passive: whoever resolves to kill him or-herself ultimately becomes one who submits passively to death and awaits its approach [36].

In his comparison between suicide and writing, writing is a form of creation and suicide is the radical decision made by any artist. Considered in this way, the character of this novel—Master Yehudi—takes the place of the artist who commits suicide, and therefore, he "submits passively to death and awaits its approach." Indeed, this thesis evokes Yehudi's last words to his disciple: "Death isn't so terrible, Walt. When a man comes to the end of the line, it's the only thing he really wants" (220). So, Master Yehudi has submitted passively to death and was waiting for its approach. Still, there are the unavoidable consequences that remain for the object created after the death of the creator. In Blanchot's words, "the work wants, so to speak, to install itself, to dwell in this *negligence*. [...] It is attracted by an ordeal in which everything is risked, by an essential risk where being is at stake, where nothingness slips away, where, that is, the right, the power to die is gambled" (Blan-

chot, *Space* 107). Taking this argument and comparing it with the Blanchotian idea of negligence, if the one who chooses voluntary death is
the one who is trying to avoid "the other death," then, in Blanchot
words, the suicidal artist is choosing a visible death "in order to exclude
the visible one" and, therefore leaves his work of art stuck in this constant negligence of visible death (107).

Throughout the third stage of the novel, Walt tries to survive in
a world that is already strange for him. At the same time, this part is
divided in two parts. Firstly, Walt goes back to vagrancy, delinquency
and even prostitution, but right after that, he becomes a Bingo boy and
things seem to improve for him. During this successful episode of his
life, he opens a nightclub called "Mr. Vertigo" and in it he starts baseball
bets. However, he still remembers Master Yehudi and insists on the
fact that although he tries hard to move on, in a way his life is miserable,
and overall he is not the same person anymore:

> It hurt too much to look back, so I kept my eyes fixed in front of me, and
> every time I took another step forward, I drifted farther away from the person
> I'd been with Master Yehudi. The best part of me was lying under the ground
> with him in the California desert. I'd buried him there along with his Spinoza,
> his scrapbook of Walt the Wonder Boy clippings, and the necklace with my
> severed finger joint, but even though I went back there every night in my
> dreams, it drove me crazy to think about it during the day. Killing Slim was
> supposed to have squared the account, but in the long run it didn't do a bit
> of good. I wasn't sorry for what I'd done, but Master Yehudi was still dead,
> and all the Bingos in the world couldn't begin to make up for him. I strutted
> around Chicago as if I were going places, as if I were a regular Mr. Somebody,
> but underneath it all I was no one. Without the master I was no one, and I
> wasn't going anywhere [240].

There is evidence that the character is still looking for Master Yehudi
as someone to control him. As the first levitating experience shows,
there is a radical abandonment of his former self to begin a transformation into another self that is, in some way, ethereal and inert and
that he can only be while he is performing his art. What remains after
that is only, as he asserts some lines after, a shadow of what he was: "I
lived like a shadow, prowling the country in search of Uncle Slim" (255),
a shadow of what he was.

Walt, as Master Yehudi's creation, installs in the negligence committed by his creator in his voluntary death in which he has to die
the death he had refused, that is, what the French critic calls "the other
death, the death one cannot grasp" (Blanchot, *Space* 106). So Walt, as

his creation, is trapped in this negligence, which is "perpetual flight and inertia" (Blanchot, *Space* 107). This feeling of loss is also depicted in a vital character of this section of the novel—Dizzy Dean—who is a baseball player that reminds him of his past self:

> If nothing else, it proves how sick my soul had become in the years since Master Yehudi's death. I'd latched onto Dizzy because he reminded me of myself, and as long as his career flourished, I could relive my past glory through him. Maybe it wouldn't have happened if he'd pitched for some town other than Saint Louis. Maybe it wouldn't have happened if our nicknames hadn't been so similar. I don't know. I don't know anything but the fact was that a moment came when I couldn't tell the difference between us anymore. His triumphs were my triumphs, and when bad luck finally caught up with him and his career fell apart, his disgrace was my disgrace [265].

The excerpt above shows Walt's nostalgia for his past self and how he still needs to relive through others those experiences that marked his life. Moreover, he searches for that missing part of him in every corner of his life and realizes that no matter what he does, that part is buried with his creator Master Yehudi. In fictional terms, Walt becomes a character who, after the loss of his creator in the imaginary space, lives in constant search of his imaginary essence and therefore survives lost in his own fictional space. Walt lives in a "perpetual flight," as Blanchot would say, but with no concrete direction.

The fourth and last part of the novel gives the protagonist the opportunity to heal his past and recover that part of him that was lost. He comes back to Cibola to live with Mrs. Whitherspoon in the same house and the same room. In other words, a perpetual return that, in relation to Blanchot, expresses the "interminable" or "incessant" that results from contact with death in the process of creation. And, in order to complete this recreation of Walt, the last pages of the book surprise the reader with the information that the author of the book *Mr. Vertigo* is Walt Rawley:

> I thought about getting away from Kansas for a few months and seeing the world, but before I could make any definite plans, I was rescued by the idea of writing this book. I can't really say how it happened. It just hit me one morning as I climbed out of bed, and less than an hour later I was sitting at a desk in the upstairs parlor with a pen in my hand, scratching away at the first sentence. I had no doubt that I was doing something that had to be done, and the conviction I felt was so strong, I realize now that the book must have come to me in a dream—but one of those dreams you can't remember that vanish the instant you wake up and open your eyes on the world [290].

In his description of the process of writing, it is curious how his way of writing is similar to that of Paul Auster using the "school composition book from the five-and-ten" (290). Nevertheless, one of the fundamental references of this last part is the fact that he mentions Daniel Quinn as the person who is going to get the manuscript and publish it, or at least "Dan will know what to do with the book I've written. He'll correct the spelling mistakes and get someone to type up a clean copy, and once *Mr. Vertigo* is published, I won't have to be around to watch the mugwumps and morons try to kill me" (290).

Daniel Quinn is a recurrent character in Auster's novels. He is the protagonist of *City of Glass* and he also appears in the last novel of the trilogy, *The Locked Room*, as the private detective who looked for Fanshawe for a period of time. Here, he is Walt's nephew and a teacher who is apparently familiarized with literature; in the first volume of the trilogy, he was a writer transformed into a private detective. The figure of Daniel Quinn is introduced right at the end of the novel in order to reinforce the cyclical effect of the narration and not only takes us back to the beginning but also to Auster's other novels, and, accordingly, opens the literary space they represent in the fiction. Finally, in his new condition as creator, Walt sees in him the ability to train and transform a new boy into the Wonder Boy; however, he ends up reflecting on the essence of the expression of inspiration:

> Deep down, I don't believe it takes any special talent for a person to lift himself off the ground and hover in the air. We all have it in us—every man, woman, and child—and with enough hard work and concentration, every human being is capable of duplicating the feats I accomplished as Walt the Wonder Boy. You must learn to stop being yourself. That's where it begins, and everything else follows from that. You must let yourself evaporate. Let your muscles go limp, breathe until you feel your soul pouring out of you, and then shut your eyes. That's how it's done. The emptiness inside your body grows lighter than the air around you. Little by little, you begin to weigh less than nothing. You shut your eyes; you spread your arms; you let yourself evaporate. And then, little by little, you lift yourself off the ground. Like so [293].

These are the last words of the novel. Explicitly, he is explaining again the process of levitation. He uses key words and expressions to describe it such as "evaporate," "your soul pouring out of you," "emptiness," or "lighter," but probably the most important one is "you must learn to stop being yourself." This line echoes Blanchot's words when he says "the work requires of the writer that he lose everything he might

143

construe as his own nature, that he lose all character" (Blanchot, *Space* 55) and together with this, the rest of the words refer to a definition of the image as it shows in the following excerpt:

> But what is the image? When there is nothing, the image finds in this nothing its necessary condition, but there it disappears. The image needs the neutrality and the fading of the world; it wants everything to return to the indifferent deep where nothing is affirmed; it tends toward the intimacy of what still subsists in the void [251].

Afterword

In this work I have studied the influence the French writer, critic and philosopher Maurice Blanchot has on the work of the American writer Paul Auster. This influence is manifested in his texts through intertextuality. In order to study the intertextual phenomenon in Auster's fiction, it is necessary to take into account three different factors proposed by Aliki Varvogli: "the writers and literary texts which appear in the books, the cultural texts of myth and history, and the relations among Auster's books themselves" (13). I have reached the conclusion that there is one more way of intertextual representation: the influence Auster's translations had on his future fiction. In chapter two I analyze Auster's literary influences and it is clear that French literature becomes one of the most relevant sources of his fiction. Apart from this, Auster also includes in his novels other influences such as the American transcendentalists, Edgar Allan Poe, Nathaniel Hawthorne, Herman Melville or even European writers such as Franz Kafka or Rainer Maria Rilke. However, the effects of Paul Auster's translations on his fiction have not been analyzed before. Certainly, Tom Theobald alludes to the connection between Auster and Blanchot and, in order to do that, he talks about Auster's work as a translator but he does not consider in his study this influence as a way of intertextuality. Translation becomes a way of influence and its effects on Auster's works are relevant for the construction of his fiction. In other words, from this intertextual influence it is possible to focus on a theoretical perspective since the knowledge of Blanchot's literary theory oriented Paul Auster in the construction of his novels. Thus, this work analyzes the influence Blanchot's theory of the space of literature has in Paul Auster's work. The five chapters included in this work deal with the construction of a literary space and how that is fictionalized in Auster's fiction.

To start with, chapter one offers an analysis of the different definitions of intertextuality and how those definitions can be connected to the influence Blanchot has on Auster's fiction. Auster's act of translation becomes an intertextual relation that consequently supports the thesis and it is through this approach with the French philosopher the way in which Auster gets to know his theory. This chapter, apart from showing how intertextual theories lead to Kristeva's final definition of intertextuality, it claims the union between intertextuality and translation as a tool for creating a space of influence. In this context, the connection between translation and intertextuality or intertextuality through the process of translation occurs from the perspective of imitation. If we consider the act of translation a process of imitation, the translator becomes a recreator, a rewriter of the source text into another language and, therefore, it becomes a way to forge his role as future writer. This is the reason why this analysis considers the role of translator from a perspective of a future writer as it is Auster's case.

Also, in this first chapter, I have concluded that the translated texts by Auster become a theoretical corpus for the construction of his fiction. In all the works he translates, "The Book of Questions," "The Last Word," "The Idyll" and "After the Fact," the most relevant ideas presented by Blanchot in his central work *The Space of Literature* are present: the concept of space, solitude, language, the act of writing and especially, the concept of inspiration. Together with this, I reach the conclusion that not only does Auster incorporate these concepts into his poetry, he also does it in his first work of non-fiction *The Invention of Solitude*. Here, in this chapter, I assert that this first work becomes a fundamental work of theory for Auster's future fiction. Actually, I consider it Auster's ars poetica since it clearly defines what solitude, writing and literature means for Auster, ideas and topics that come up recurrently in his works and especially in the ones analyzed here.

The second chapter of this work deals with Blanchot's concept of inspiration, a fundamental step in the whole process of writing. In his theoretical project, Blanchot explains the idea of inspiration by a reinterpretation of the myth of Orpheus and Eurydice. Contrary to most of the traditional studies of the myth which focus on what it is considered Orpheus' mistake in his desperate turning back to see his lover, Blanchot claims this event crucially positive. In other words, Orpheus's mistake would explain the artist's longing and dependence on his work of art. It is necessary that Orpheus turns and causes Eurydice's disappearance since Blanchot understands Orpheus as the creator who creates through his art an object that in this case is Eurydice. Her disappearance is compared to the transformation of the signifier into the signified and, therefore, into an invisible concept. Thus, from this perspective, Orpheus's mistake is necessary for the work of art to be accomplished. Together with this, the existence of a vanishing Eurydice, a kind of specter, represents the idea of the double introduced by Blanchot. In this context, the double only emerges as long as the writer, in the intimacy of his solitude, starts the task of writing. This is what Blanchot calls "someone else" that appears when the writer is writing. Thus, Eurydice stands for this double that always mirrors the activity of the creator. Furthermore, the space left between Orpheus and Eurydice in the transformation is what Blanchot calls the orphic space and it is the realm in which the work of art, in this case literature, can be accomplished.

The next three chapters deal with Auster's novels *Ghost, The Music of Chance* and *Mr. Vertigo*, which are analyzed in this work as fictionalizations of the idea of inspiration. In chapter three, I introduce a study of *Ghosts*, the second novel of *The New York Trilogy*. In it, Auster fictionalizes the creation of a literary space through the plot of a detective case and to characters whose only tasks are observation and writing. As in the other two chapters, inspiration is the main topic of the novel shown in the relationship of the two characters. Throughout the novel, Black is an implicit inspiration for Blue, that being so, everything that Blue writes in his notes is inspired by Blue and viceversa. The space that separates them, the distance between the two windows, is the orphic space that at the end stands for the literary space they both are creating which culminates in Black's room. Clearly, both Blue and Black become doubles that feed the fictional space.

Chapter four is dedicated to the novel *The Music of Chance*, a novel that does not deal with writing but with two characters trapped in a world created by others. In this context, this novel is the result of a process of inspiration in which the two central characters, condemned to pay a debt through the construction of an absurd wall, become the creations of two other characters. In this particular case, the creators, despite the fact that they are present at the beginning of the novel, seem to be unapproachable entities or specters that exist distantly from the two central characters, who are the ones that carry out the whole plot. Certainly, the orphic space becomes the caravan where they live and the wall they have to construct, an implicit symbol of language and writing. Also, as another characteristic of this study, they cannot abandon this place as creations. If they do, they risk their lives and that is what happens to one of the characters. Finally, the protagonist abandons this place but his life out of the orphic space is short and he disappears immediately.

The last chapter introduces *Mr. Vertigo*, the story of a man who trains a child to teach him how to fly. Inspiration is symbolized in this novel by the figure of the two central characters, the master and the student, in other words, the creator and the object created. Throughout the novel, the child is transformed into a different person in order to learn how to fly and this transformation turns him into his master's creation. In this sense, the idea of inspiration is reflected in the act of levitation and how this practice turns the object into an image especially bearing in mind that the boy, through the act of flying, becomes something similar to a specter. His existence changes every time he flies and when he flies he is positioned in a sort of limbo that is no more than the representation of the orphic space. Again, master and student become doubles as the novel finishes with the flying boy turned into a writer—a creator just as his master was.

This work opens a new perspective in the academic criticism of Paul Auster's fiction by focusing the attention on intertextuality and especially in the influence French writers have in his oeuvre. It offers a comparative study with the writer Maurice Blanchot and a new interpretation that distances Auster's fiction from the previous critical proposals. Thus, Auster's fiction becomes the construction and fictionalization of a literary space as a celebration of the act of creation.

Chapter Notes

Introduction

1. These letters now belong to the Paul Auster archive in the Berg Collection at the New York Public Library.
2. *L'Espace littéraire* (1955).
3. *Faux Pas* (1943).
4. *La Part de feu* (1949).
5. *Le Livre à venir* (1959).
6. *L'Entretien infini* (1969).

Chapter 1

1. Auster writes about many different personal experiences in his non-fictional works such as *The Art of Hunger and Ohter Essays* (1982), *The Invention of Solitude* (1982), *The Red Notebook* (1995), and *Hand to Mouth* (1997).
2. Maurice Blanchot sent Paul Auster four letters between 1975 and 1981. These letters are in the Paul Auster archive in the Berg Collection at the New York Public Library. Mainly the letters discuss Blanchot's recommendations for the translation of his texts. Apart from that, we can read in them Blanchot's comments and thoughts about Auster's first poetry, evidence of a short but significant literary relationship.
3. See Kristeva 93.
4. The manuscript of this interview belongs to the Paul Auster archive: "Interview with Edmond Jabès," Box 8/Folder 1, Paul Auster archive, Berg Collection, New York Public Library.
5. These letters can be found in the Paul Auster archive in the Berg Collection at the New York Public Library. I

would like to thank Paul Auster and Anne Garner for arranging my visit there. I had the opportunity to review the writer's manuscripts, materials and letters with him.

6. In 1942 Albert Camus published *The Myth of Sisyphus*, a reinterpretation of the Greek myth in terms of its absurdity and how this new condition affected modern times. Basically, Camus rewrites the Greek myth in order to explain the absurd existence of the modern individual. Only one year later, in 1943, Maurice Blanchot published his book *Faux Pas*, a collection of essays which includes a text dedicated to this myth and a reflection of Camus's text. Although "The Idyll" was written and published some years earlier, there is an absurd atmosphere that governs the story in relation to the existential condition of the modern man.

7. Some critics understand the trilogy as an existential quest such as Allison Russell in her essay "Deconstructing *The New York* Trilogy: Paul Auster's Anti-Detective Fiction" (1990). Also Anne M. Holzapfel studies the whole trilogy as a deconstruction of the detective genre in her work *The New York Trilogy: Whodunit?* (1996).

8. Novels like *The New York Trilogy* use the room as an essential space for the characters to develop their literary tasks. Daniel Quinn, in *City of Glass*, finishes his investigation locked in a room. In fact, the third novel of the volume is titled *The Locked Room*. Also, *Travels in the Scriptorium* situates its ac-

tion in the reduced space of a room from which the central character cannot go out. Rooms in Auster are mainly related to the act of writing creation.

9. The last section of *The Space of Literature* is dedicated to Hölderlin and is titled "Hölderlin's Itinerary," a study of Hölderlin's poetry and as a result, a reflection on inspiration in relation to literature.

10. This is something that Nietzsche already expressed in one of his works *On Truth and Lying in a Non-Moral Sense* (1873). In this work, Nietzsche explains how the human being, in his necessity to live integrated in society, uses language to designate things and he describes this act as the first impulse towards truth. Nietzsche defines the word as the reproduction of the sound of a nervous impulse and this impulse is in charge of defining the causes that live outside us. Nonetheless, he explains that the word is not able to express the essence and truth of things because when we speak we think that we can posses what we are expressing with our voices but we just own the metaphors of which we are uttering. Thus, man is constructing his truth and the truth of his world with a nervous impulse, an image, and a sound. In this process of representing the world, the word becomes a concept in the moment in which it stops designating one individual experience to name a group of similar experiences that will never be identical (Nietzsche, *Tragedy* 145).

11. In his work *Maurice Blanchot: The Refusal of Philosophy* (1997), Gerald L. Bruns dedicates a chapter to what he titles "The Theory of Writing." In this section, he discusses the concept of essential solitude and the relevance of Levinas's expression of the *il y a* in Blanchot's theory. To some extent, as he explains, the concept of the *il y a* is intimately related with the idea of the subject and consequently to the idea of the other. Bruns also asserts, "In fasci-

nation, the subject is reduced to a pure passivity where subjectivity suffers a reversal, a dispossession, as if stolen away" (Bruns 60). Again, the idea of losing the essence of the individual to turn into someone else becomes relevant in the definition of Levinas's *il y a* and, in a way, one of its main messages.

12. I would like to remark that it is crucial to connect both Blanchot's and Auster's influences. While Blanchot uses Mallarmé's poetry to develop a theory of language and writing, Mallarmé becomes one of Auster's greatest influences. The French symbolists had an essential impact on Auster's former texts, yet Mallarmé's influence plays a greater role as Auster translated one of Mallarmé's most major works *A Tomb for Anatole* (*Pour un tombeau d'*Anatole, translated by Paul Auster and published by North Point Press in 1983), a collection of poems dedicated to Mallarmé's sick and finally dead son. Some critics believe that the introduction of conflicts between father and son in Auster's fiction have been partly inspired by this text. The loss of a son is explicitly mentioned in *City of Glass*, and in *The Invention of Solitude*, the relationship between father and son is implied through the absence of the paternal figure creating a conflict for the narrator. In this context, Mallarmé becomes a link between the two writers: both were influenced by Mallarmé's works.

13. In relation to the definition of language see Michel Foucault *Maurice Blanchot: The Thought from the Outside* (2006).

14. For a further analysis of Blanchot's idea of death in language and literature see Haase and Large, 43–48.

15. In relation to this, Roland Barthes describes the "the zero degree of writing" as "the negative momentum, and an inability to maintain it (writing) within time's flow, as if literature [...] could no longer find purity anywhere but in the absence of all signs, finally

proposing the realization of this Or-phean dream: a writer without literature" (Barthes, *Degree* 11). In response to Barthes's definition of the "degree zero of writing," Blanchot comments: "Roland Barthes perhaps also designated the moment when literature might be grasped. But the fact is that at that point it would be not only a bland, absent and neutral writing, it would be the very experience of "neutrality" (Blanchot, *Book* 209).

16. In his work *Maurice Blanchot: The Refusal of Philosophy* (2005) Gerald L. Bruns explains that the concept of writing, in the context of Kafka's work, is a demand and a way of "relocating the origin of writing outside the writer" (Bruns 62). Also, Bruns tries to explain writing as the bearer of impossibility trapped in an extreme experience which, at the same time, is an original event. Both Bruns and Blanchot believe in the exigency of writing. Bruns explains this as if we could "imagine writing as an invasion of the writer by this impossibility" (Bruns 62–63).

17. Roland Barthes, in *The Death of the Author* (1967), uses Mallarmé's work as the source and example for his theories. In his discussion, he affirms that it is the work of the French poet which helps to formulate a new way of perceiving literature and writing in which the figure of the artist is erased in favor of language. That is, Barthes writes, "For him, for us, it is language which speaks, not the author; to write is, through a prerequisite impersonality to reach that point where only language acts, 'performs,' and not 'me'" (Lodge 168). Another relevant influence in Blanchot's thesis is the essay "What Is an Author?" (1969) by Michel Foucault. In it he states that "the writing subject cancels out the signs of his particular individuality. As a result, the mark of the writer is reduced to nothing more than the singularity of his absence; he must assume the role of the dead man in the game of writing" (Lodge 205).

18. In this respect, Blanchot asserts that "art is experience because it is experimental: because it is a search-an investigation which is not undetermined but is, rather, determined by its indeterminacy, and involves the whole of life" (Blanchot, *Space* 89). Besides, Blanchot's hypothesis about experience encloses a paradox that conditions both the work and the writer, writing that "the work itself is by implication an experience of death which he apparently has to have been through already in order to reach the work and, through the work, death" (Blanchot, *Space* 93).

Chapter 2

1. "When I am alone, I am not alone, but in this present, I am already returning to myself in the form of Someone. Someone is there, where I am alone. The fact of being alone is my belonging to this dead time which is not my time, or yours, or the time we share in common, but Someone's time. Someone is what is still present when there is no one" (Blanchot, *Space* 31).

2. At the beginning of *The Space of Literature* Blanchot states, "The work requires of the writer that he loses everything he might construe as his own 'nature,' that he loses all character and that, ceasing to be linked to others and to himself [...] he becomes the empty place where the impersonal affirmation emerges" (Blanchot, *Space* 55).

3. Also, Clark compares Blanchot's "notion of literature as a total experience" with the early Heidegger and his concept of anxiety. For the German philosopher and in Clark's words, anxiety is "a shattering of human being, a crisis of the human essence" (Clark 240). Concretely, he concludes that "anxiety is a mood in which whomever it possesses is anxious about the totality of existence as the question of its own contingency, and about death as the possibility of the impossibility of existing" (240).

4. In relation to this contrast between day and night, Gerald L. Bruns defines Orpheus's task as the action "to bring light out of darkness," that is "to bring Eurydice into the daylight, to make the daylight more luminous through the visibility of Eurydice" and in this sense he concludes that "the task of Orpheus [...] is to make truth radiant. This is the meaning of Eurydice or the work of art: the radiance of truth" (Bruns 70).

5. The literary critic Manuel Asensi formulates an argument to explain Blanchot's thesis and concludes that literature goes constantly back to reality in the same way Eurydice tries to come back to life. Concretely, he defines literature as a "vampire" of reality (Asensi, "Vampiros" 76).

6. As stated by Gerald L. Bruns the "entre-temps" is "the between-time, that occurs when Orpheus turns his forbidden look toward Eurydice" and it is in that space when Orpheus suffers an uncontrollable desire that goes beyond his need to posses his lover, "it is as though Orpheus were responding to a deeper claim, an exigency more powerful than his essentially philosophical task of restoring Eurydice to the light of being. This would be the exigency of writing" (Bruns 70). In this context, Bruns proposes the space of the "between-time" as the space of writing and Orpheus's attraction towards Eurydice as the intense impulse of writing creation.

7. In the chapter "The Trace of Trauma: Blindness, Testimony and the Gaze in Blanchot and Derrida," Michael Newman outlines a similar reflection to the one presented by Clark about Blanchot's reinterpretation of Orpheus's myth. Like Clark, Newman focuses his analysis on Orpheus's aim that essentially becomes to reach the origin of the work of art. Newman states that Orpheus's labor consists in "bringing the 'other night,' the 'obscure point,' back to the light of day." In his own words, "by Blanchot's 'other night' we may under-

stand the night which withdraws from the dialectical opposition of day and night and which, as the murmur of unnegatable being, is linked with the *il y a*." Again, the central thesis of Newman's discussion, as in Clark, is Orpheus's failure. He justifies Blanchot's thesis in the following way: "if Orpheus would have failed by succeeding, by bringing the object of his desire to the light of day precisely as an object produced by work, according to Blanchot he in a certain sense succeeds by failing, or more specifically by *forgetting*" (Gill 158).

8. According to Leslie Hill, Orpheus's mistake or act of betrayal as he calls it "is a response to another more demanding requirement, to the law of the origin and of worklessness itself which asserts that what is essential is not the work, but the darkness without which there would be no work at all" (119). Hill's argument would also justify Eurydice's tendency of disappearance and the attraction towards an origin that apparently only hides absence.

9. According to Leslie Hill, the neuter displaces the function of words so "they cease to mean what they mean, but begin to oscillate uncontrollably between what they still do mean and the always other possibility that they mean something different, something that inhabits them as their own fundamental alterity" (133). This statement would explain Blanchot's thesis that the neuter "lets us feel that what is being recounted is not being recounted by anyone: it speaks in the neutral," an aspect that opens the possibility of the alterity, that is, a "someone" that "falls into self-nonidentification" (Blanchot, *Conversation* 384). As Leslie Hill adds, the neuter is "presence deferred and dispersed, transformed into a possibility of otherness" (Hill 133).

10. Michael Newman interprets this extract in the following way: "Narcissus falls in love with his image because he is oblivious to that otherness in himself

which cannot be seen. The blind spot of vision is associated here with that place where the subject is touched by both death and the other" (Gill 153).

Chapter 3

1. Most of the critical work dedicated to analyze *The New York Trilogy* considers it an example of anti-detective fiction. Such is the case of Anne M. Holzapfel who in her book *The New York Trilogy: Whodunit?* (1996) discusses *Ghosts* and its central character as being modeled after the hard-boiled detective novel structure (57).

2. Ilana Shiloh in her book *Paul Auster and Postmodern Quest*, compares Blue's activity of looking to Sartre's existentialist philosophy. She mentions specifically Sartre's work *Being and Nothingness* (1943) in which the look is the primary means by which the subject establishes his relationship with the other. The other's look is indispensable to the individual's existence, which constitutes for himself through human interaction (61). Sartre's existential theory is more focused on a social relationship based on the acceptance of the other and the existential consequences that confrontation has. Blanchot's theory is more metaphysical; he does not understand the gaze as a way of accepting the other but rather as a way of finding another part of the self which takes the form of a double in the work of fiction. There is no social interaction for either Blanchot or Auster; it is a metaphysical encounter with the individual's inside.

3. Paul Jahshan in his essay "Paul Auster's Specters," affirms that the function of the mirror put up by White between Blue and Black establishes a relationship between writing and itself, between reading and itself, between a signifier and itself. He also adds that Blue feels alienated from a meaning (Black), which is to be gained (395).

4. Clara Sarmento in her essay "Paul

Auster's The New York Trilogy: The Linguistic Construction of an Imaginary Universe" (2002) states that "to enter Black's room is like entering and unraveling a mystery as if entering Black's own mind, the last redoubt to be explored in this endless play of looks" (93).

Chapter 4

1. Critics such as Tim Woods, Eyal Dotan or Warren Oberman write about the novel as if it were a clear example of the effect of capitalism in postmodern society and how Auster uses gambling and gaming, considered some of the main consequences of capitalism, as a metaphor to create a fictional world.

2. On the contrary, Tom Theobald structures the novel in three different and "inter-related stages of awareness": driving across America, the poker game, and the construction of the wall. These three different stages are based on an existentialist reading of the text in terms of the existentialist freedom and responsibility of the character (86). The three stages that Theobald mentions are extremely relevant considering the construction of the wall as the most significant. However, whereas the wall becomes a literary symbol, especially bearing in mind that it has been an image that Auster has used throughout his poetry as he does in the collection "Wall Writing," the other two stages can be considered more a rite of passage or a necessary moment of revelation the character goes through conditioned by the postmodern society he lives in. Therefore, Theobald stages work correctly from a postmodernist existential reading of the text while the other moments which are the separation from his world—the encounter with Pozzi and the arrival to the millionaires' house— also constitute an existential reading of the text but from a more literary perspective.

3. This image is comparable to the

narrator's situation with Fanshawe in *The Locked Room*. When describing his double Fanshawe, the narrator says that the only way he could imagine him was locked and alone in a room and finally concludes that "this room, I now discovered, was located inside my skull" (Auster, *Trilogy* 293).

4. Like in other works, this is the case of Fanshawe or even Mr. White in *Ghosts*: the supposed creators are figures who seem distant from the action. Characters become puppets controlled by almost invisible puppeteers who participate in the action but whose role in it, in most of the cases, is almost circumstantial. There is something some of them share in common, and it is the fact that they are presented as dressed in white. In the case of *City of Glass*, Peter Stillman Jr. is described as a semi-dead individual, almost a ghost whose white clothing contributes to enhance this image. Clearly, Peter Stillman Jr. is not the creator of Daniel Quinn´s fiction, however, it is true that he is the one who takes the private detective to a fictional world, that is, the fake detective case, from which he is not able to escape. In *Travels of the Scriptorium*, Mr. Blank would be another example. Always dressed in white, his role of creator is central to turn it upside down and transform him into a character or victim of his own characters.

5. This situation has been illustrated in other Auster novels. In *The Locked Room* the narrator desperately looks for Fanshawe in an unconscious act of killing his own creator. A similar situation takes place in *Travels in the Scriptorium* when Mr. Blank's characters are trying to kill him.

6. Aliki Varvogli analyzes the contrast between journeys and confined spaces first on a simply level and considers it to be a representation of "Nashe's changing fortunes, his movement from freedom to captivity, from self-determination to submission." However, on a deeper, theoretical level, this opposition "is also a metaphor for the act of writing, the interplay between the personal, the intense concentration on the part of the writer, and the metaphorical journey of his imagination" (107).

7. Objects are fundamental in Auster's fiction, especially in relation to the use they have. In *City of Glass*, Peter Stillman, Sr., presents a significant reflection of an umbrella and the use it performs. In *Travels in the Scriptorium*, all the objects of Mr. Blank's apartment are labeled with their names so it is possible to identify them with their definition and concept, that is, the signifier with its signified.

8. There is a parallelism between the loss of meaning and function of the stones and the umbrella episode in *City of Glass*. Peter Stillman Sr., in a conversation with Daniel Quinn, reflects on the fact that objects, when they no longer perform their function, are not the same objects anymore: "Because it can no longer perform its function, the umbrella has ceased to be an umbrella. It might resemble an umbrella, it might once have been an umbrella, but now it has changed into something else. The word, however, has remained the same. Therefore, it can no longer express the thing" (77–78).

Chapter 5

1. The idea of the American identity is linked to another novel, *City of Glass*, and Peter Stillman, Sr.'s project of the creation of a new America through the recuperation of the original language of Eden. In relation to this, Auster presents the idea of the American Dream as a genuine characteristic of American society and American identity.

2. In relation to this, Aliki Varvogli suggests that "the father-son relationship once again concerns a surrogate, rather than a biological, father" and "the theme continues with the rigorous training with which the master effects the little boy's transformation" (158).

154

3. In *The Locked Room*, the narrator's intention is to find his creator Fanshawe and at some point kill him. Still, this is absolutely impossible and it is only almost at the end of the novel that they have an encounter behind a door but they never see or touch each other. Something similar occurs in *Ghosts*, with the relationship between Black and Blue since Blue finally kills Black, abandons the room and the novel finishes.

Bibliography

Primary Sources: Works by Paul Auster (in Chronological Order)

NOVELS

Squeeze Play. New York: Alpha-Omega Books, 1982.

City of Glass. Los Angeles: Sun & Moon Press, 1985.

Ghosts. Los Angeles: Sun & Moon Press, 1986.

The Locked Room. Los Angeles: Sun & Moon Press, 1986.

The New York Trilogy. London: Faber & Faber, 1987.

In the Country of Last Things. New York: Viking, 1987.

Moon Palace. New York: Viking, 1989.

The Music of Chance. New York: Viking, 1990.

Leviathan. New York: Viking, 1992.

Mr. Vertigo. London: Faber & Faber, 1994.

Timbuktu. London: Faber & Faber, 1999.

The Book of Illusions. London: Faber & Faber, 2002.

Oracle Night. New York: Henry Holt, 2003.

The Brooklyn Follies. London: Faber & Faber, 2005.

Travels in the Scriptorium. New York: Henry Holt, 2006.

Man in the Dark. New York: Henry Holt, 2008.

Invisible. London: Faber & Faber, 2009.

Sunset Park. New York: Henry Holt, 2010.

SCREENPLAYS

Smoke. London: Faber & Faber, 1995.

Blue in the Face. London: Faber & Faber, 1995.

Lulu on the Bridge. New York: Henry Holt, 1998.

The Inner Life of Martin Frost. London: Faber & Faber, 2007.

NON-FICTION

"Interview with Edmond Jabès." 1978. Box 8/Folder 1. Berg Collection. Paul Auster Archive. New York Public Library.

White Spaces. Barrytown, New York: Station Hill, 1980.

The Art of Hunger and Other Essays. London: The Menard Press, 1982.

The Invention of Solitude. New York: Sun Press, 1982.

Ground Work: Selected Poems and Essays. London: Faber & Faber, 1990.

The Art of Hunger: Essays, Prefaces, Interviews. Los Angeles: Sun & Moon Press, 1992.

The Red Notebook. London: Faber & Faber, 1995.

Hand to Mouth. New York: Henry Holt, 1997.

Collected Prose. London: Faber & Faber, 2003.

Winter Journal. New York: Henry Holt, 2012.

Report from the Interior. London: Faber & Faber, 2013.

Here and Now. Letters: 2008–2011. Paul Auster & J.M Coetzee. New York: Viking Penguin, 2013.

POETRY

Unearth. Weston, CT: Living Hand, 1974.
Wall Writing. Berkeley: The Figures, 1976.
Effigies. Paris: Orange Export Ltd., 1977.
Fragments from Cold. Brewster, New York: Parenthèse, 1977.
Facing the Music. Barrytown, New York: Station Hill, 1980.
Disappearances: Selected Poems. Woodstock, New York: The Overlook Press, 1988.

TRANSLATIONS

Miró Sculptures. Minneapolis: Walker Art Center, 1971.
A Little Anthology of Surrealist Poems. New York: Siamese Banana Press, 1972.
Fits and Starts: Selected Poems of Jacques Dupin. Salisbury, Wilts: Living Hand, 1973.
Saul Friedländer & Mahmoud Hussein. Arab & Israelis: A Dialogue. New York: Holmes & Meier, 1975.
Miró: Painting & Sculpture 1969–74. New York: Pierre Matisse Gallery, 1975.
Marc Chagall: The Four Seasons. New York: Pierre Matisse Gallery, 1975.
Hantaï: Paintings Watercolors 1971–75. New York: Pierre Matisse Gallery, 1975.
The Uninhabited: Selected Poems of André du Bouchet. New York: Living Hand, 1976.
Marc Chagall: A Celebration. New York: Pierre Matisse Gallery, 1977.
Jean-Paul Sartre. Life/Situations. New York: Pantheon Books, 1977.
Jean Chesneaux. China from The 1911 Revolution to Liberation. New York: Pantheon Books, 1977.
Alain Bouc. Mao Tse-Tung: A Guide to His Thought. New York: St. Martin's Press, 1977.
The Penguin Book of Women Poets. London: Allen Lane, 1978.

Jean Chesneaux. China: The People's Republic, 1949–76. New York: Pantheon Books, 1979.
Georges Simenon. African Trio: Talatala, Tropic Moon, Aboard the Aquitaine. New York: Harcourt Brace Jovanovich, 1979.
Stéphane Mallarmé: Selected Poetry and Prose. New York: New Directions, 1982.
The Notebooks of Joseph Joubert: A Selection. San Francisco: North Point Press, 1983.
Stéphane Mallarmé: A Tomb for Anatole. San Francisco: North Point Press, 1983.
Philippe Petit: On the High Wire. New York: Random House, 1985.
Maurice Blanchot. Vicious Circles: Two Fictions & "After the Fact." Barrytown, New York: Station Hill, 1985.
Miró/Artigas: Terres de Grand Feu. New York: Pierre Matisse Gallery, 1985.
Joan Miró: Selected Writings and Interviews. Boston: G.K Hall & Co., 1986.
Joan Miró: A Restrospective. New York: Solomon R. Guggenheim Museum/ Yale University Press, 1987.
Selected Poems of René Char. New York: New Directions, 1992.
Jacques Dupin: Selected Poems. Winston-Salem: Wake Forest University Press, 1992.

BOOKS EDITED WITH CONTRIBUTIONS

Living Hand # 1. Paris: Living Hand, 1974.
Ex Libris I: Major Movements of 20th Century Art. New York: Ex Libris, 1974.
Ex Libris 2: Dada and Duchamp. New York: Ex Libris, 1975.
Jean-Paul Riopelle: Paintings from 1974 and Pastels from 1975. New York: Pierre Matisse Gallery, 1975.
Living Hand #4. New York: Living Hand, 1975.
The Thirteen Woman and Other Stories. New York: Living Hand, 1976.

158

Allen Mandellbaum. Leaves of Absence.
  New York: Living Hand, 1976.
Sarah Plimpton. Single Skies. New York:
  Living Hand, 1976.
*Younger Critics of North America: Essays
  on Literature and the Arts.* Fairwater,
  WI: Tom Montag/Margins, 1976.
*Voices within the Ark: The Modern
  Jewish Poets.* New York: Avon Books,
  1980.
*Young Voices in American Poetry 1980:
  An Anthology.* Corte Madera, CA:
  Harbinger Press, 1980.
Homage to Mandelstam. Cambridge,
  UK: Los Poetry Press, 1981.
*The Random House Book of Twentieth
  Century French Poetry.* New York:
  Random House, 1982.
Charles Reznikoff: Man and Poet. Orono:
  University of Maine/National Poetry
  Foundation, 1984.
The Sin of the Book: Edmond Jabès. Lin-
  coln: University of Nebraska Press,
  1985.
21+1 American Poets Today. Montpel-
  lier, France: Delta, 1986.
Orange Export Ltd. 1969–1986. Paris:
  Flammation, 1986.
*The Pushcart Prize XI: Best of The Small
  Presses.* Wainscott, New York: Push-
  cart Press, 1986.
The Selected Poems of Edmond Jabès.
  Barrytown, New York: Station Hill,
  1988.
Letters to a Bookstore & Co. 1978–88.
  New York: Books & Co., 1988.
*Translating Poetry: The Double
  Labyrinth.* London: Macmillan, 1989.
*Brushes with Greatness: An Anthology of
  Chance Encounters with Celebrities.*
  Toronto: Big Bang Books/Coach
  House Press, 1989.
*A Literary Christmas: Great Contempo-
  rary Christmas Stories.* New York: At-
  lantic Monthly Press, 1992.
The Poetry of Anthony Barnett. Lewes,
  UK: Allardyce Books, 1993.
True Tales of American Life. New York:
  Henry Holt, 2001.

Primary Sources: Works by Maurice Blanchot (in Chronological Order of French Release)

Theoretical Works

Faux Pas. Paris: Éditions Gallimard,
  1943.
Faux Pas. Trans. Charlotte Mandell.
  Stanford: Stanford University Press,
  2001.
La part du feu. Paris: Éditions Gallimard,
  1949.
The Work of Fire. Trans. Charlotte Man-
  dell. Stanford: Stanford University
  Press, 1995.
L'Éspace littéraire. Paris: Éditions Galli-
  mard, 1955.
The Space of Literature. Trans. and
  intro. Ann Smock, 1989.
Le livre à venir. Paris: Éditions Galli-
  mard, 1959.
The Book to Come. Trans. Charlotte
  Mandell. Lincoln: University of Ne-
  braska Press, 2003.
L'Entretien infini. Paris: Éditions Galli-
  mard, 1969.
The Infinite Conversation. Trans. and
  foreword Susan Hanson. Minneapolis:
  University of Minnesota Press, 2003.
L'Amitié. Paris: Éditions Gallimard, 1971.
Friendship. Trans. Elizabeth Rottenberg.
  Stanford: Stanford University Press,
  1997.
L'Ecriture du désastre. Paris: Éditions
  Gallimard, 1980.
The Writing of the Disaster. Trans. Ann
  Smock. Lincoln: University of Ne-
  braska Press, 1995.
La Communauté Inavouable. Paris: Les
  Ediditions de Minuit, 1983.
The Unavowal Community. Trans. Pierre
  Joris. Barrytown, New York: Station
  Hill, 1988.
Une voix venue d'ailleurs. Paris: Éditions
  Gallimard, 2002.
The Station Hill Blanchot Reader. Bar-
  rytown, New York: Station Hill, 1999.

FICTION

Thomas l'obscur. Paris: Éditions Gallimard, 1941.

Aminadab. Paris: Éditions Gallimard, 1942.

L'Arrêt de mort. Paris: Éditions Gallimard, 1948.

Le Tres-Haut. Paris: Éditions Gallimard, 1949.

Le Pas au-delá. Paris: Éditions Gallimard, 1973.

L'Instant de ma mort. Paris: Éditions Gallimard, 1994.

Secondary Sources

Addy, Andrew. "Narrating the Self: Story-Telling as Personal Myth-Making in Paul Auster's *Moon Palace.*" *Arts, Littératures & Civilisations du Monde Anglophone* 6 (1996).

Alford, Steven E. "Chance in Contemporary Narrative." *Paul Auster.* Ed. Harold Bloom. Philadelphia: Chelsea House, 2004. 113–135.

Allen, Graham. *Intertextuality.* New York: Routledge, 2011.

Andrews, Corey. "The Subject and the City: The Case of the Vanishing Private Eye in Paul Auster's *City of Glass.*" *Henry Street* 6.1 (1997): 61–72.

Asensi, Manuel. *Historia de la teoría de la literatura. Vol.II, El Siglo XX hasta los años setenta.* Valencia: Tirant lo Blanc, 2003.

_____. "Vampiros y literatura: la teoría en la literatura de Maurice Blanchot." *Revista Anthropos. Maurice Blanchot. La escritura del silencio* 192–193. Rubí: Anthropos Editorial, 2001. 67–77.

Bakhtin, Mikhail. *The Dialogic Imagination: Four Essays.* Austin: University of Texas Press, 1982.

_____. "From the Prehistory of Novelistic Discourse." *Modern Criticism and Theory: A Reader.* Ed. David Lodge. Essex, UK: Longman, 1990.

_____. *Marxism and the Philosophy of Language.* Cambridge: Harvard University Press, 1986.

Baldick, Chris. *Concise Dictionary of Literary Terms.* London: Oxford University Press, 1996.

Ballesteros González, Antonio. *Narciso y el doble en la literatura fantástica victoriana.* Cuenca: Universidad de Castilla La Mancha, 1998.

_____. *Vampire Chronicle. Historia natural del vampiro en la literatura anglosajona.* Zaragoza: unaLuna Ediciones, 2000.

Barone, Dennis, ed. *Beyond the Red Notebook: Essays on Paul Auster.* Philadelphia: University of Pennsylvania Press, 1995.

Barthes, Roland. "The Death of the Author." *Modern Criticism and Theory: A Reader.* Ed. David Lodge. Essex, UK: Longman, 1990.

_____. *Image Music Text.* London: HarperCollins, 1977.

_____. *A Roland Barthes Reader.* Ed. and introd. Susan Sontag. London: Vintage Classics, 2000.

_____. *Writing Degree Zero.* Trans. from the French by Annette Lavers and Colin Smith. London: Jonathan Cape, 1967.

Bassnet, Susan, and Peter Bush. *The Translator as Writer.* London: Continuum, 2006.

Bawer, Bruce. 2004. "Doubles and More Doubles." *Paul Auster.* Ed. Harold Bloom. Philadelphia: Chelsea House, 2004.

Beckett, Samuel. *Collected Shorter Plays.* London: Faber & Faber, 1984.

_____. *The Grove Centenary Edition: Poems, Short Fiction, Criticism.* Ed. Paul Auster. New York: Grove Press, 2006.

_____. *Samuel Beckett Trilogy: Molloy, Malone Dies, The Unnamable.* London: Calder Publications, 2003.

Ben-Zvi, Linda, and Angela Moorjani. *Beckett at 100. Revolving It All.* New York: Oxford University Press, 2008.

Bernstein, Stephen. "Auster's Sublime

Clousure: *The Locked Room." Beyond the Red Notebook: Essays on Paul Auster.* Ed. Denis Barone. Philadelphia: University of Pennsylvania Press, 1995.

Bloom, Harold, ed. *The Anxiety of Influence.* New York: Oxford University Press, 1997.

_____, ed. *Paul Auster.* Philadelphia: Chelsea House, 2004.

Bradbury, Malcolm. *Introduction to American Studies.* Harlow: Longman, 1998.

_____. *The Modern American Novel.* Oxford: Oxford University Press, 2009.

Brown, Mark. *Paul Auster. Contemporary American and Canadian Novelists.* Manchester: Manchester University Press, 2007.

Bruckner, Pascal. "Paul Auster, or The Heir Intestate." *Beyond the Red Notebook: Essays on Paul Auster.* Ed. Denis Barone. Philadelphia: University of Pennsylvania Press, 1995.

Bruns, Gerald L. *Maurice Blanchot: The Refusal of Philosophy.* Baltimore: John Hopkins University Press, 2005.

Butler, Martin, and Jens Martin. "The Poetics and Politics of Metafiction: Reading Paul Auster´s *Travels in the Scriptorium.*" *English Studies* 89, no. 2 (2008): 195–209.

Campbell, Julie. "Becket and Paul Auster: Fathers and Sons and the Creativity of Misreading." *Beckett at 100: Revolving it All.* Ed. Linda Ben-Zevi and Angela Moorjani. New York: Oxford University Press, 2008.

Camus, Albert. *The Myth of Sisiphus.* New York: Vintage, 1991.

Chenetier, Marc. *Beyond Suspicion: New American Fiction Since 1960.* Liverpool: Liverpool University Press, 1996.

_____. *Critical Angles: European Views of Contemporary American Literature.* Carbondale: Southern Illinois University Press, 1986.

_____. "Paul Auster's Pseudonymous World." *Beyond the Red Notebook.* Philadelphia: University of Pennsylvania Press, 1995.

Ciocia, Stefania, and Jesús A. González, eds. *The Invention of Illusions: Perspectives on Paul Auster.* Newcastle Upon Tyne: Cambridge Scholars, 2011.

Clark, Timothy. *The Theory of Inspiration: Composition as Crisis of Subjectivity in Romantic and Post-Romantic Writings.* Manchester: Manchester University Press, 1997.

Cohen, Josh. *Interrupting Auschwitz: Art, Religion, Philosophy.* London: Continuum, 2005.

Cohn, Dorrit. "Metalepsis and Mise en Abyme." *Narrative* 20, no. 1 (2012): 105–114.

Crasnow, Ellman, and Philip Haffenden. "New Founde Land." *Introduction to American Studies.* Harlow: Longman, 1998.

Currie, Mark. *Postmodern Narrative Theory.* New York: Palgrave Macmillan, 2011.

Dällenbach, Lucien. *The Mirror in the Text.* Trans. Jeremy Whiteley with Emma Hughes. Oxford: Polity Press, 1989.

Davis, Paul. "The Work and the Absence of the Work." *Maurice Blanchot: The Demand of Writing.* Ed. Carolyn Bailey Gill. New York: Routledge, 1996.

De Certeau, Michel. *The Practice of Everyday Life.* Berkeley: University of California Press, 1998.

Donovan, Christopher. 2005. *Postmodern Counternarratives: Irony and Audience in the Novels of Paul Auster, Don Delillo, Charles Johnson, Tim O'Brien.* New York: Routledge.

Dotan, Eyal. "The Game of Late Capitalism: Gambling and Ideology in *The Music of Chance.*" *Mosaic: A Journal for the Interdisciplinary Study of Literature* 33, no. 1 (2000): 161–177.

Dow, William. "Paul Auster's *The Invention of Solitude*: Glimmers in a Reach to Authenticity." *Paul Auster.* Ed. Harold Bloom. Philadelphia: Chelsea House, 2004.

161

Bibliography

Drenttel, William. *Paul Auster: A Comprehensive Bibliographic Checklist of Published Works 1968–1994*. New York: The Delos Press, 1994.

Ellmann, Maud. *The Hunger Artists: Starving, Writing and Imprisonment*. London: Virago Press, 1993.

Ford, Mark. "Inventions of Solitude: Thoreau and Auster." *Journal of American Studies* 33, no. 2 (1999): 201–220.

Foucault, Michel. *Maurice Blanchot: The Thought from Outside*. Trans. Jeffrey Mehlman and Brian Massumi. New York: Zone Books, 2006.

_____. *The Order of Things*. London: Routledge, 2002.

_____. "What Is an Author?" *Modern Criticism and Theory: A Reader*. Ed. David Lodge. Essex, UK: Longman, 1990.

Genette, Gérard. *Narrative Discourse. An Essay in Method*. Trans. Jane E. Lewin, foreword Jonathan Culler. Ithaca: Cornell University Press, 1983.

Geraci, Ginevra. "A Writer in Recoil: The Plight of Mankind and the Dilemma of Authorship in Paul Auster's *Travels in the Scriptorium*." *The Invention of Illusions: International Perspectives on Paul Auster*. Ed. Stefania Ciocia and Jesús A. González. Newcastle Upon Tyne: Cambridge Scholars, 2011.

Gill, Carolyn Bailey. *Maurice Blanchot: The Demand of Writing*. New York: Routledge, 1996.

Gregg, John. *Maurice Blanchot and the Literature of Transgression*. Princeton: Princeton University Press, 1994.

Haase, Ullrich, and William Large. *Maurice Blanchot* (Routledge Critical Thinkers). New York: Routledge, 2001.

Hamsun, Knut. *Hunger*. Trans. from the Norwegian by Sverre Lyngstad, introd. Jo Nesbo, afterword Paul Auster. Edingburgh: Cannongate Books Ltd., 2011.

Hassan, Ihab Habib. *The Dismemberment of Orpheus: Toward a Postmodern Literature*. Madison: University of Wisconsin Press, 1982.

Haus, Andreas. *The Implosion of Negativity. The Poetry and Early Prose of Paul Auster*. Norderstedt: Books on Demand GmbH, 2010.

Hawthorne, Nathaniel. *Collected Novels*. New York: The Library of America, 1983.

_____. *Selected Tales and Sketches*. New York: Penguin, 1987.

Herzogenrath, Bernd. *An Art of Desire: Reading Paul Auster*. Amsterdam: Rodopi, 1999.

Hill, Leslie. *Blanchot: Extreme Contemporary*. London: Routledge, 1997.

Hollier, Denis. *Absent Without Leave. French Literature Under the Threat of War*. Cambridge: Harvard University Press, 1997.

Holzapfel, Anne M. *The New York Trilogy: Whodunit?* Berlin: Peter Lang AG, 1996.

Iyer, Lars. "There Is Language: Speech and Writing in Blanchot." *Parallax* 12, no. 2 (2006): 83–97.

Jahshan, Paul. 2004. "Paul Auter's Specters." *Journal of American Studies* 37, no. 3 (2004): 389–405.

Kaufman, Eleanor. "Midnight, and the Inertia of Being." *Parallax* 12, no. 2 (2006): 98–111.

Kristeva, Julia. *Desire in Language: A Semiotic Approach to Literature and Art*. New York: Columbia University Press, 1980.

Kušnir, Jaroslav. *American Fiction: Modernism-Postmodernism, Popular Culture and Metafiction*. Stuttgart: Ibidem, 2005.

Lavender, William. "The Novel of Critical Engagement: Paul Auster's *City of Glass*." *Paul Auster*. Ed. Harold Bloom. Philadelphia: Chelsea House, 2004.

Lodge, David, ed. *Modern Criticism and Theory. A Reader*. Essex, UK: Longman Group, 1990.

López García, Dámaso. *Sobre la Imposibilidad de la Traducción*. Cuenca: Universidad de Castilla La Mancha, 1991.

Mallarmé, Stéphane. *A Tomb for Anatole.* Trans. and introd. Paul Auster. New York: New Directions, 2005.

Mallia, Joseph. "Interview with Joseph Mallia." *The Red Notebook.* Paul Auster. London: Faber & Faber, 1995.

Martin, Brendan. *Paul Auster's Postmodernity.* London: Routledge, 2008.

McCaffery, Larry, and Sinda Gregory. 1995. "Interview with Larry McCaffery and Sinda Gregory." *The Red Notebook.* Paul Auster. London: Faber & Faber, 1995.

Megill, Allan. *Prophets of Extremity: Nietzsche, Heidegger, Foucault, Derrida.* Berkeley: University of California Press, 1985.

Melville, Herman. *Billy Budd and Other Stories.* New York: Penguin, 1986.

Nealon, Jeffrey T. "Work of the Detective, Work of the Writer: Paul Auster's *City of Glass.*" *Modern Fiction Studies* 42, no. 1 (Spring 1996): 91–110.

Newman, Michael. "The Trace of Trauma: Blindness, Testimony and the Gaze in Blanchot and Derrida." *Maurice Blanchot: The Demand of Writing.* Ed. Carolyn Bailey Gill. New York: Routledge, 1996.

Nicol, Bran. *The Cambridge Introduction to Postmodern Fiction.* Cambridge: Cambridge University Press, 2009.

Nietzsche, Friedrich. *The Birth of the Tragedy and Other Texts.* Texts in History and Philosophy. Cambridge: Cambridge University Press, 1999.

———. *Early Greek Philosophy and Other Essays.* New York: Russell & Russell, 1964.

———. *The Will to Power.* New York: Vintage, 1968.

Oberman, Warren. "Existentialism Meets Postmodernism in Paul Auster's *The Music of Chance.*" *Critique* 45, no. 2 (2004): 191–206.

Ovid. *Metaphorphoses.* Trans. A.D. Melville. New York: Oxford University Press, 1998.

Patterson, Richard F. 2008. "The Teller's Tale: Text and Paratext in Paul Auster's *Oracle Night.*" *Critique* 49, no. 2 (2008): 115–128.

Peacock, James. *Understanding Paul Auster.* Columbia: University of South Carolina Press, 2010.

Pirandello, Luigi. *Six Characters in Search of an Author.* Trans. and introd. Stephen Mulrine. London: Nick Hern Books, 2003.

Poe, Edgar Allan. *The Fall of the House of Usher and Other Writings.* London: Penguin Classics, 2003.

Poole, Steven. 2006. "Ghosts in the Machine." *New Statement Magazine* 30 October 2006.

Rodríguez-Gago, Antonia. "Re-Figuring the Stage Body through the Mechanical Reproduction of Memory." *Beckett at 100: Revolving It All.* Ed. Linda Ben-Zevi and Angela Moorjani. New York: Oxford University Press, 2008.

Ropars-Wuilleumier, Marie-Claire. "On Unworking: The Image in Writing According to Blanchot." *Maurice Blanchot: The Demand of Writing.* Ed. Carolyn Bailey Gill. New York: Routledge, 1996.

Rubin, Derek. "'The Hunger Must Be Preserved at All Cost': A Reading of *The Invention of Solitude.*" *Beyond the Red Notebook: Essays on Paul Auster.* Ed. Denis Barone. Philadelphia: University of Pennsylvania Press, 1995.

Rudman, Mark. "Paul Auster: Some 'Elective Affinities.'" *Review of Contemporary Fiction* 14, no. 1 (1994): 44–48.

Russel, Allison. "Deconstructing *The New York Trilogy*: Paul Auster's Anti-Detective Fiction." *Critique: Studies in Contemporary Fiction* 31, no. 2 (1990): 71–85.

Sarmento, Clara. "Paul Auster's *The New York Trilogy*: The Linguistic Construction of an Imaginary Universe." *Interdisciplinary Literary Studies: A Journal* 3, no. 2 (2002): 82–101.

Saussure, Ferdinard. 1966. *Course in*

General Linguistics. New York: McGraw-Hill, 1966.

Shakespeare, William. *Complete Works of William Shakespeare: The Alexander Text.* London: Collins, 2006.

Shelley, Mary. *Frankenstein.* London: Penguin Popular Classics, 1994.

Shiloh, Ilana. *Paul Auster and Postmodern Quest: On the Road to Nowhere.* New York: Peter Lang, 2002.

Shostak, Debra. "Under the Sign of *Moon Palace*: Paul Auster and the Body in Text." *Critique* 49, no. 2 (Winter 2008): 149–168.

Sorapure, Madeleine. "The Detective and the Autor: City of Glass." *Beyond the Red Notebook: Essays on Paul Auster.* Philadelphia: University of Philadelphia Press, 1995. 71–87.

Springer, Carsten. *Crises: The Works of Paul Auster.* Frankfurt: Peter Lang, 2001.

_____. *A Paul Auster Sourcebook.* Frankfurt: Peter Lang, 2001.

Theobald, Tom. *Existentialism and Baseball: The French Philosophical Roots of Paul Auster.* Saarbrücken: Lambert Academic, 2010.

Thoreau, David Henry. 1986. *Walden and Civil Disobedience.* London: Penguin Classics, 1986.

Tysh, Chris. "From One Mirror to Another: The Rhetoric of Disaffiliation in *City of Glass.*" *Review of Contemporary Fiction* 14, no. 1 (1994): 46–53.

Unamuno, Miguel de. *Niebla.* Madrid: Cátedra, 2010.

Varvogli, Aliki. "Ailing Authors: Paul Auster´s *Travels in the Scriptorium* and Philip Roth's *Exit Ghost.*" *Review of International American Studies: On Terror and Security* (special issue), 3.3–4.1 (Winter 2008/Spring 2009): 94–100.

_____. "Exploding Fictions": *Paul Auster.* Ed. Harold Bloom. Philadelphia: Chelsea House, 2004.

_____. *The World That Is the Book. Paul Auster´s Fiction.* Liverpool: Liverpool University Press, 2001.

_____. "The Worst Possibilities of the Imagination Are the Country You Live In." *The Invention of Illusions: International Perspectives on Paul Auster.* Ed. Stefania Ciocia and Jesús A. González. Newcastle upon Tyne: Cambridge Scholars, 2011.

Venuti, Lawrence. "Translation, Intertextuality, Interpretation." *Romance Studies* 27, no. 3 (2009): 157–173.

Wall, Thomas Carl. *Radical Passivity: Levinas, Blanchot and Agamben.* Albany: State University of New York Press, 1999.

Weisenburger, Steven. "Inside *Moon Palace.*" *Beyond the Red Notebook: Essays on Paul Auster.* Philadelphia: University of Pennsylvania Press, 1995.

Wells, H.G. *The Invisible Man.* London: Penguin Classics, 2012.

Woods, Tim. "*The Music of Chance*: Aleatorical (Dis)Harmonies Within "The City of the World." *Beyond the Red Notebook: Essays on Paul Auster.* Philadelphia: University of Pennsylvania Press, 1995.

Worton, Michael, and Judith Still. *Intertextuality: Theories and Practices.* Manchester: Manchester University Press, 1993.

Zeigler, Heide. "A Room of One's Own: The Author and Reader in the Text." *Critical Angles: European Views of Contemporary American Literature.* Carobondale: Southern Illinois University Press, 1986.

Zilcosky, John. "The Revenge of the Author: Paul Auster's Challenge to Theory." *Critique* 39, no. 3 (1998): 195–207.

Index

Index

Ghosts 83, 87, 101
Ghosts 4, 7, 56, 74–92, 99, 147, 153, 154, 155, 157
Gill, Carolyn Bailey 73, 152, 153, 161, 162
Gregg, John 140, 162

Haase, Ullrich 150, 162
Hamsun, Knut 162
Hassan, Ihab Habib 66, 67, 68, 162
Haus, Andreas 162
Hawthorne, Nathaniel 7, 87, 145, 162
Hercules (mythological character) 128
Herzogenrath, Bernd 162
Hill, Leslie 37, 63, 152, 162
Hölderlin, Friedrich 9, 14, 34, 150
Holzapfel, Anne M. 149, 153, 162
Hunger 97

Identity 3, 22, 23, 41, 73, 84, 98, 99, 100, 101, 104, 119, 125–128, 132, 139, 154
The Idyll 2, 18, 21, 25, 146, 149
Image 10, 11, 16, 26, 31, 32, 42, 43, 44, 45, 48, 61, 62, 63, 64, 65, 68, 69, 70, 72–76, 78, 79, 84, 102, 103, 135, 136, 137, 144, 148, 150
Imaginary 5, 13, 26, 34, 42, 44, 47, 48, 54, 62, 69, 70, 94, 95, 95, 102, 105, 106, 108, 109, 110, 111, 112, 115, 117, 118, 119, 121, 122, 123, 126, 127, 138, 139, 142, 153, 163
In the Country of Last Things 22, 157
Incessant 41, 47, 48, 58, 75, 90, 124, 139, 142
Infinite 44, 63, 79
The Infinite Conversation 4, 53, 59, 63, 160
Infinite movement 39, 53, 59, 92
Influence 2, 7, 8, 9, 11, 14, 16, 18, 29, 37, 145, 146, 148, 150, 151
Inner essence 132, 133
Inner experience 38, 43, 44, 59
Inner self 77, 128, 129, 130, 132
Inner space 32, 43, 44, 53, 54, 55
Inner world 32, 33, 34
Inspiration 2, 4, 5, 47, 50, 56, 57, 58, 59, 60, 65, 66, 68, 69, 70, 72, 74, 76, 77, 79, 81, 82, 86, 91–97, 99, 100, 104, 110, 112, 115, 118, 122, 124, 125, 126–133, 136, 143, 146, 147, 148, 150
Interiority 53, 54, 55, 75, 76
Interminable 40, 41, 42, 43, 47, 48, 75, 76, 89, 139, 142
Intertextuality 3, 7–16, 145, 146, 148, 160
Intimacy 39, 43, 52, 53, 55, 62, 69, 88, 144, 147
The Invention of Solitude 8, 29, 31, 157, 161

Invisible 18, 31, 32, 53, 54, 55, 58, 62, 63, 72, 75, 79, 80, 88, 123, 139, 147
Invisible 157
Invisibility 30, 34, 37, 50, 53, 54, 75, 76, 88
Iyer, Lars 162

Jabès, Edmond 2, 9, 14, 16, 17, 18, 157, 159
Jahshan, Paul 153, 162
Joubert, Joseph 9, 14, 158

Kafka, Franz 9, 14, 37, 41, 49, 50, 51, 52, 145, 151
Kaufman, Eleanor 162
Kristeva, Julia 9, 10, 11, 12, 13, 14, 146, 149, 162
Kusnir, Jaroslav 162

Language 1, 3, 4, 10, 11, 12, 13, 15, 18, 19, 21, 25, 26, 27, 28, 30, 32, 35, 36, 39, 41, 42, 44–52, 53, 54, 55, 57, 58, 60, 62, 63, 67, 68, 79, 80, 84, 97, 99, 101, 102, 105, 112, 113, 114, 118, 128, 132, 133, 146, 148, 150, 151, 154
The Last Word 2, 18, 25, 146
Lavender, William 162
Letters (from Maurice Blanchot to Paul Auster) 2, 9, 18–20, 149, 157, 159
Leviathan 4, 22, 157
Limit experience 38, 59, 60
Literary death 50, 54, 74, 101, 121
Literary space 1, 3, 4, 11, 13, 26, 30, 34, 37, 38, 39, 40, 41, 43, 44, 45, 47, 49, 50, 54, 58, 59, 60, 61, 62, 65, 71, 74, 93, 97, 101, 105, 107, 109, 111, 117–121, 123, 124, 130, 143, 145, 147, 148, 149, 152, 159
Lodge, David 11, 151, 160, 162

Mallarmé, Stéphane 9, 14, 37, 45, 46, 47, 50, 150, 151, 158, 163
Mallia, Joseph 163
Man in the Dark 157
Martin, Brendan 161, 163
McCaffery, Larry 163
Megill, Allan 163
Melville, Herman 145, 163
Memory 28, 29, 30, 34, 35, 36, 37, 57, 96, 116, 117, 122, 163
Metafiction 3, 85, 161, 165
Mise en abyme 29, 107
Mr. Vertigo 4, 5, 56, 108, 125–144, 147, 148, 157
Modernism 1, 14, 66, 68
Moon Palace 22, 127, 157, 160, 164
Multicultural 1, 125
Multiculturalism 125

166